INTRODUCTION
TO THE DWELLING PLACES
OF
THE INTERIOR CASTLE
OF
SAINT TERESA OF AVILA

by
Otger Steggink, O. Carm.

CARMELITE MEDIA

Translation by Pegasus Translation (Tucson, Arizona)
Layout and Cover Design: William J. Harry, O. Carm.

Carmelite Media
8501 Bailey Road
Darien, Illinois 60561

Phone: 1-630-971-0724
Website: carmelites.info/publications

Originally published by the *Centre d'Etudes d'Histoire de la
Spiritualité* (C.E.H.S.) within the *Parole et Silence Series* of
the *Collection Grands Carmes* under the title *Introduction au
Château intérieur de Sainte Thérèse d'Avila.*

ISBN of French Edition: 2-84573-522-7
© Editions Parole et Silence, 2006

ISBN of Current English Edition: 978-1-936742-12-7

Table of Contents

I. Why This Book by Saint Teresa?

Of all the saint's writings, this work has a systematic and universal intention and quality. It is her most balanced work, integrating the ascetic life and the mystical life.

In addition, of all the Teresian writings (the doctrinal writings), *The Interior Castle* is chronologically the last. This is the book of Saint Teresa's spiritual maturity. *The Interior Castle* is complementary to the other books. Here the saint returns to the rich treasure of experiences related in *The Book of My Life*, *The Way of Perfection* and *The Spiritual Testimonies* (or *The Favors of God*) to present them in a less personal and less descriptive form.

The Interior Castle is related in particular to *The Book of Her Life* (her autobiography), written fifteen years before, and returns to and develops her fundamental intuitions. In fact, its purpose is to perfect and complete her first treatise.

II. The Conception and Origin of the Book

There are three possible explanations for the conception and origin of *The Interior Castle*:

- A strictly supernatural origin
- A strictly natural origin
- A theory of mixed origin

Diego de Yepes (friend, confessor and later biographer of Saint Teresa) cites as the origin of the comparison between a castle and *The Interior Castle*, a vision Teresa had on the feast of the Holy Trinity at the time she was starting to write about prayer. This account cannot be doubted. Nevertheless, if God grants us visions, it is through images that the subject has previously acquired. Hence, let us not exclude the

supernatural, which truly influenced the conception
of the book. However, there is also a deep and slowly
developing origin of the book.

We should add that the image of the castle may have
been inspired by the novels of chivalry that Teresa read
in her youth. Three literary types are found in these
books: the knight, the lady and the castle. The lady the
knight must win is located in the castle. Francisco de
Ribera, Saint Teresa's first biographer, says that in her
youth she wrote a novel of chivalry. The text of this
book has not been preserved and the influence of this
youthful experience could only have been secondary.

To account for the conception and origin of *The
Interior Castle*, it is necessary to go very far back in Saint
Teresa's internal life. We must first determine what ideas
The Interior Castle are based on so we can then show how
many of the preceding currents of Teresian thought are
in harmony with the book and lead up to it.

From the literary point of view, there are three
elements on which *The Interior Castle is* based: castle,
soul and God. God lives in the center of the castle, or,
without the allegory, at the core of the soul. We find a
pronounced insistence on these concepts of God and
soul, in the idea of the Trinity living within the soul.
These ideas were already found in the saint's earlier
works.

Thus, it is important, as an introduction to reading *The
Interior Castle*, to take a look at this theme in the earlier
works. Her are a few quotations:

> The most we have to strive for in the beginning is
> to care for oneself alone and consider that there is
> nothing on earth but God and oneself-- and this
> practice is very beneficial.[1]

---

1. Teresa de Avila, *Book of Her Life*, Chapter 13:9. Unless otherwise
noted, the text of St. Teresa's writings is taken from the translation by Kieran

> Let nothing trouble you,
>
> Let nothing scare you,
>
> All is fleeting,
>
> God alone is unchanging.
>
> Patience
>
> Everything obtains.
>
> Who possesses God
>
> Nothing wants
>
> God alone suffices.[2]

You already know that God is everywhere. It's obvious, then, that where the king is, there is his court; in sum, wherever God is, there is heaven. Without a doubt you can believe that where His Majesty is present, all glory is present. Consider what St. Augustine says, that he sought Him in many places but found Him ultimately within himself. Do you think it matters little for a soul with a wandering mind to understand this truth and see that there is no need to go to heaven in order to speak with one's Eternal Father or find delight in Him? Nor is there any need to shout. However softly we speak, He is near enough to hear us. Neither is there any need for wings to go to find Him. All one need do is go into solitude and look at Him within oneself, and not turn away from so good a Guest but with great humility speak to Him as to a father. Beseech Him as you would a father; tell Him about your trials; ask Him for a remedy against them, realizing that you are not worthy to be His daughter.[3]

Once while I was reciting with all the Sisters the hours of the Divine Office, my soul suddenly

---

Kavanaugh and Otilio Rodriguez, The Collected Works of *St. Teresa of Avila, Vol. One,* (ICS Publications, Institute of Carmelite Studies, Washington, D.C., 1976).

  2. *Poems. Efficacy of Patience*, Vol. Three

  3. *The Way of Perfection*, Chapter 28:2 (vol. 2, pp. 140-141).

withdrew into meditation; and it seemed to me
to be like a brightly polished mirror, without
any part on the back or sides or top or bottom
that wasn't totally clear. In its center Christ, our
Lord, was shown to me, in the way I usually see
Him. It seemed to me I saw Him clearly in every
part of my soul, as though in a mirror. And this
mirror also—I don't know how to explain it—was
completely engraved upon the Lord Himself by
means of a very loving communication.[4]

I think this vision is advantageous to persons
withdrawn into contemplation, in teaching them
to consider the Lord as very deep within their
souls; such a thought is much more alluring and
fruitful than thinking of Him as outside oneself,
as I mentioned at other times. And some books
on prayer tell about where one must seek God.
Particularly, the glorious St. Augustine speaks
about this for neither in the market place not in
pleasures nor anywhere else that he sought God
did he find Him as he did when he sought Him
within himself. Within oneself, very clearly, is the
best place to look; and its not necessary to go to
heaven, not any further than our own selves; for
to do so is to tire the spirit and distract the soul,
without gaining as much fruit.[5]

In Teresa's thought, the concept of the soul for the
spiritual life is one of the concepts that is strongly
developed as she progresses in her spiritual life. A short
time before *The Interior Castle* was written, she wrote to
Father Gracián: "I understand better every day... what a
soul represents to God."[6]

---

4. *Book of Her Life*, Chapter 40:5 (vol. 1, p. 356). [Throughout the English
version of St. Teresa's writings, the original translator has used the English
words "recollect" and "recollection" to translate the Spanish words "recogerse"
and "recogemiento." We believe "withdraw into meditation (or contemplation)"
and "withdrawal into meditation (or contemplation)" represent a more accurate
rendering of the original and have changed the quotations accordingly.]

5. *Book of Her Life*, Chapter 40:6 (vol. 1, p. 357).

6. *Letters* (translator's translation).

It is not possible to follow this development in detail. We will limit ourselves to presenting here quotations from earlier works that prepare the fundamental concept of the book, i.e. the quotations that evoke the spirit of the Castle as faithfully as possible.

> Now to return to what I was saying, I would like to know a way of explaining how this holy fellowship with our Companion, the Saint of saints, may be experienced without any hindrance to the solitude enjoyed between the soul and its Spouse when the soul desires to enter this paradise within itself to be with its God and close the door to all the world. I say "desires" because you must understand that this withdrawal into contemplation is not something supernatural, but that it is something we can desire and achieve ourselves with the help of God—for without this help we can do nothing, not even have a good thought. This withdrawal into contemplation is not a silence of the faculties; it is in an enclosure of the faculties within the soul.[7]

> Those who by such a method can enclose themselves within this little heaven of our soul, where the Maker of heaven and earth is present, and grow accustomed to refusing to be where the exterior senses in their distraction have gone or look in that direction should believe they are following an excellent path and that they will not fail to drink water from the fount; for they will journey far in a short time. Their situation is like that of a person who travels by ship; with a little wind he reaches the end of his journey in a few days. But those who go by land take longer.[8]

> He so esteems our soul that He doesn't allow it to be occupied with things that can harm it during the time He wishes to favor it. Rather, He

---

7. *The Way of Perfection*, Chapter 29:4 (vol. 2 pp. 146-147).
8. *The Way of Perfection*, Chapter 28:5 (vol. 2 pp. 141-142).

immediately places it near Himself and shows
it in an instant more truths, and gives it clearer
understanding of what everything is, than we
could have here below in many years. For our eyes
don't see clearly; the dust blinds us as we walk. By
this living water the Lord brings us to the end of
the journey without our understanding how.[9]

The concept of the presence of God in the soul,
the idea that interests us most, was for Teresa a true
discovery:

In the beginning I was ignorant about a certain
matter because I didn't know that God was in all
things, and though He seemed so present to me,
I thought this omnipresence was impossible. I
couldn't stop believing that He was there since
it seemed to me that I understood almost clearly
that He was there by His very presence. Those
who had no learning told me that He was present
only by grace. I couldn't believe this, because, as I
say, it seemed to me He was present; and so I was
troubled. A learned man from the order of the
glorious St. Dominic freed me from this doubt,
for he told me that God was present and of how
God communicates Himself to us; these truths
consoled me tremendously. It should be noted
and understood that this heavenly water, this
magnificent favor from the Lord, always leaves
great fruits in the soul as I shall now explain.[10]

The importance of this discovery to St. Teresa is
difficult to assess. There is a very close connection
between this passage and another in *The Interior Castle*.

I know a person who hadn't learned that God was
in all things by presence, power, and essence, and
through a favor of this kind that God granted her
she came to believe it. After asking a half-learned

9. *The Way of Perfection*, Chapter 19:7 (vol. 2, p. 110).
10. *Book of Her Life*, Chapter 18:15 (vol. 1, p 163).

man of the kind I mentioned—he knew as little as she had known before God enlightened her—she was told that God was present only by grace. Such was her own conviction that even after this she didn't believe him and asked others who told her the truth, with which she was greatly consoled.[11]

The personal value she placed on this discovery is interesting in this case: "…these truths consoled me tremendously" and "…the truth, with which she was greatly consoled."

The statements in the *Spiritual Testimonies* are equally powerful:

1575, SEVILLE

Once while I was withdrawn into contemplation in this company I always bear with me in my soul, God seemed so present to me that I thought of St. Peter's words: You are Christ, Son of the Living God. For God was thus living in my soul. This presence is not like other visions, because it is accompanied by such living faith that one cannot doubt that the Trinity is in our souls by presence, power, and essence. It is an extremely beneficial thing to understand this truth. Since I was amazed to see such majesty in something so lowly as my soul, I heard: "It is not lowly daughter, for it is made in My image." I also understand some things about why God delights to be with souls more than with other creatures. These matters were so subtle that even though my intellect understood them immediately, I shall not be able to explain them.[12]

This event is of such importance in the history of St. Teresa's ideas and it is so closely linked to the leading idea of the *Interior Castle* that it compels us to assign

---

11. *The Interior Castle, Fifth Dwelling Place*, Chapter 1:10 (vol. 2, pp. 339-340).

12. *Spiritual Testimonies* #49 (vol. 1, p. 413).

secondary importance to the other elements. Let us just note the sense of interiorization that St. Teresa gives to prayer. Here are a few quotations:

> I spoke of the significance of entering within ourselves to be alone with God. [13]

> By turning my gaze just a little inward to behold the image I have in my soul…[14]

> Neither is there any need for wings to go to find Him. All one need do is go into solitude and look at Him within oneself …[15]

We are principally interested in the mystical graces that concern the Trinity (or God) in the soul, as they are presented in the *Spiritual Testimonies* received between 1571 and 1575, i.e. in the period immediately preceding the writing of the *Interior Castle*.

1571, AVILA, ST. JOSEPH MONASTERY

> On the Tuesday following Ascension Thursday, having remained a while in prayer after Communion, I was grieved because I was so distracted I couldn't concentrate. So I complained to the Lord about our miserable nature. My soul began to enkindle, and it seemed to me I knew clearly in an intellectual vision that the entire Blessed Trinity was present. In this state my soul understood by a certain kind of representation (like an illustration of the truth), in such a way that my dullness could perceive, how God is three and one. And so it seemed that all three Persons were represented distinctly in my soul and that they spoke to me, telling me that from this day I would see an improvement in myself in respect to three things and that each one of these Persons would grant me a favor; one, the favor of charity;

---

13. *Way of Perfection*, chapter 35:1.
14. *Book of Her Life*, chapter 37:4.
15. *Way of Perfection*, chapter 28, 2

another, the favor of being able to suffer gladly;
and the third, the favor of experiencing this charity
with an enkindling in the soul. I understood
those words the Lord spoke, that the three divine
Persons would be with the soul in grace, for I saw
them within myself in the way described.[16]

JUNE 30, 1571, MEDINA DEL CAMP

I have experienced this presence of the three
Persons, which I mentioned at the beginning, up to
this day which is the feast of the Commemoration
of St. Paul. They are very habitually present in
my soul. Since I was accustomed to experience
only the presence of Jesus, it always seemed to
me there was some obstacle to my seeing three
Persons, although I understand there is only one
God. And the Lord told me today while I was
reflecting upon this that I was mistaken in thinking
of things of the soul through comparison with
corporeal things, that I should know that these
spiritual things are very different and that the soul
is capable of great rejoicing. It seemed to me there
came the thought of how a sponge absorbs and
is saturated with water; so, I thought, was my soul
which was overflowing with that divinity and in a
certain way rejoicing within itself and possessing
the three Persons.

I also heard the words: "Don't try to hold Me
within yourself, but try to hold yourself within
Me." It seemed to me that from within my soul—
where I was these three Persons present—these
persons were communicating themselves to all
creation without fail, nor did they fail to be with
me.[17]

Here the presence of the Trinity is perceived as an
inner "dwelling place", in the words of the Gospel.
The saint indicates the effectiveness of withdrawing

16. *Spiritual Testimonies* #13 (vol. 1, p. 391).

17. *Spiritual Testimonies* #14 (vol. 1, pp. 392-393).

into contemplation of this grace. A real deepening of
the Trinitarian mystery is addressed, although it is still
perceived within the soul.

SEPTEMBER 22, 1572

One day, after the feast of St. Matthew, being in
the state I'm usually in since I've seen the vision
of the Blessed Trinity and how it dwells in a soul
in the state of grace, a very clear understanding
of this mystery was granted to me so that in
certain ways and through comparisons I beheld it
in an imaginative vision. Although at other times
knowledge of the Blessed Trinity was given me
through an intellectual vision, the truth, after a few
days, no longer remained with me so that I could
think about it and find consolation in it, as I can
now.[18]

1575, SEVILLE

One time I understood how the Lord was present
in all things, and how [he is] in the soul, and
I thought of the example of a sponge which
absorbs water.[19]

1575, SEVILLE

One day after having received Communion, I
truly thought my soul was made one with the
most sacred Body of the Lord. He appeared to
me and by His presence caused me to make much
progress.[20]

We see how the saint strongly insists on the
effectiveness of the vision and of the permanent
experience of the Trinity in the soul.

But we find an elaboration of the doctrine in the *Way
of Perfection* (chapter XXVIII, No. 9-12), which is really a

---

18. *Spiritual Testimonies* #29 (vol. 1, p. 400).
19. *Spiritual Testimonies* #40 (vol, 1, p. 410).
20. *Spiritual Testimonies* #44 (vol. 1, p. 411).

first draft or sketch for the book *The Interior Castle*:

> Well, let us imagine that within us is an extremely
> rich palace, built entirely of gold and precious
> stones; in sum, but for a lord such as this. Imagine,
> too, as is indeed so, that you have a part to play in
> order for the palace to be so beautiful; for there
> is no edifice as beautiful as is a soul pure and
> full of virtues. The greater the virtues the more
> resplendent the jewels. Imagine, also, that in this
> palace dwells this mighty King who has been
> gracious enough to become your Father; and that
> He is seated upon an extremely valuable throne,
> which is your heart.[21]

> This may seem not relevant at the beginning; I
> mean, this image I've used in order to explain
> withdrawal into contemplation. But the image
> may be very helpful—to you especially—for since
> we women have no learning, all of this imagining
> is necessary that we may truly understand that
> within us lies something incomparably more
> precious than what we see outside ourselves. Let's
> not imagine that we are hollow inside. And please
> God it may be only women that go about forgetful
> of this inner richness and beauty. I consider it
> impossible for us to pay so much attention to
> worldly things if we take the care to remember we
> have a Guest such as this within us, for we then
> see how lowly these things are next to what we
> possess within ourselves.[22]

> You will laugh at me, perhaps, and say that what
> I'm explaining is very clear, and you'll be right;
> for me, though, it was obscure for some time. I
> understand well that I had a soul. But what this
> soul deserved and who dwelt within it I did not
> understand because I had covered eyes with the

---

21. *Way of Perfection*, Chapter 28:9 (vol. 2, pp. 143-144).

22. *Way of Perfection*, Chapter 28:10 (vol. 2, p. 144). [At the beginning of the
quote, we have changed "trifling" to "not relevant" to reflect better the Spanish
word *impertinente*.]

vanities of the world. For, in my opinion, if I had
understood as I do now that in this little palace of
my soul dwelt so great a King, I would not have
left Him alone so often. I would have remained
with Him at times and striven more so as not to
be so unclean. But what a marvelous thing, that
He who would fill a thousand worlds and many
more with His grandeur would enclose Himself
in something so small! [And so He wanted to
enclose Himself in the womb of His most Blessed
Mother.] In fact, since He is Lord He is free to do
what He wants, and since He loves us He adapts
Himself to our size.[23]

So that the soul won't be disturbed in the
beginning by seeing that it is too small to have
something so great within itself, the Lord doesn't
give it this knowledge until He enlarges it little by
little and it has the capacity to receive what He will
place within it. For this reason I say He is free to
do what He wants since He has the power to make
this palace a large one. The whole point is that
we should give ourselves to Him with complete
determination, and we should empty the soul in
such a way that He can store things there or take
them away as though it were His own property.[24]

This series of spiritual texts, written by St. Teresa
before *The Interior Castle*, is clear evidence that the latter
work is the final fruit of the saint's spiritual and mystical
process.

Before approaching the words of *The Interior Castle*, we
must consider what is the book's general idea, its overall
viewpoint. That is, we are led to wonder about the
book's structure and its guiding ideas. What was the goal
that St. Teresa set for herself in writing this new book
about prayer? Who is it addressed to?

23. *Way of Perfection*, Chapter 28:11 (vol. 2, p. 144).
24. *Way of Perfection*, Chapter 28:12 (vol. 2, pp. 144-145).

These are questions that can be answered by describing the composition of the book, the writing process and the book's structure.

III. The Composition, Writing Process and Structure of *The Interior Castle*

On May 28, 1577, a spiritual meeting took place between Mother Teresa of Jesus and Father Gracián de la Madre de Dios, Provincial of the Carmelite Sisters and of the Discalced Carmelites. Discussing with him certain aspects of her soul, Teresa expressed to him words of regret about her autobiography, which she had written 15 years earlier and which was in the hands of the Inquisition. Father Gracián suggested that she write another book. This was the authorization she needed to put down on paper the multitude of ideas that had been accumulating in her spirit since the image of the castle had come to her.

When she began writing *The Interior Castle*, she was 62 years old and had attained her full maturity in all respects. Fifteen years had passed since she wrote her autobiography (in 1562) and 13 years since the first edition of *Way of Perfection*. For the last five years she had fully enjoyed the mystical life and personally experienced the state of spiritual marriage.

What was needed was a complement to *Way of Perfection*. It was not enough to suggest to the souls the contemplative ideal. To teach them the way that leads to divine intimacy was not enough. Guidance must be given to those whom God has led onto that mysterious path of contemplation. They must be helped to gain the maximum profit from this heavenly favor and cautioned about possible illusions. No one was more suited to do this than the saint herself. No one was more experienced in the ways of prayer.

On the Day of the Holy Trinity, June 2, 1577, in
a solitary but pleasant cell in the Toledo Monastery,
Teresa begins to write, in her strong and large hand,
The Mansions of The Interior Castle. She had been living
cloistered in the monastery for almost a year at the
order of the Carmelite Prior General, John-Baptist
Rossi. At this time we are in the very center of the
storm that is shaking the Teresian reform to its
foundations. Long past are the times when the Prior
General was pleased to call Teresa his "daughter."[25]
At this time, deceived by inaccurate information, he
became severe and dissatisfied. Teresa's heart is weeping.
Alas, this is only the beginning. Soon the storm will
rage and the reform will be in grave danger. It is at this
very moment that she builds her Castle. She will finish
it in Avila, in November of the same year, four days
before John of the Cross, confessor of the Monastery
of the Incarnation in the same city, was seized by force
and locked up in a dark prison cell in the house of the
Carmelite friars of Toledo. The book, written in the
midst of this turmoil, is one of marvelous serenity.

PROLOGUE

THE INTERIOR CASTLE or THE DWELLING PLACES

Jhs

Teresa of Jesus, a nun of Our Lady of Mount
Carmel, wrote this treatise for her Sisters and
daughters, the Discalced Carmelite nuns.[26]

THE INTERIOR CASTLE

Jhs

---

25. *The Book of Her Foundations*, Chapter 22:1.
26. These lines in St. Teresa's own hand, appear at the beginning of the
autograph manuscript.

Not many things that I have been ordered to do under obedience have been as difficult for me as is this present task of writing about prayer. First, it doesn't seem the Lord is giving me either the spirit or the desire to undertake the work. Second, I have been experiencing now for three months such great noise and weakness in my head that I've found it a hardship even to write concerning necessary business matters. But knowing that the strength given by obedience usually lessens the difficulty of things that seem impossible, I resolved to carry out the task very willingly, even though my human nature seems greatly distressed. For the Lord hasn't given me so much virtue that my nature in the midst of its struggle with continual sickness and duties of so many kinds doesn't feel strong aversion toward such a task. May He, in whose mercy I trust and who has helped me in other more difficult things so as to favor me, do this work for me.[27]

I don't think I have much more to say than what I've said in other things they have ordered me to write; rather, I fear that the things I write about will be nearly all alike. I'm, literally, just like the parrots that are taught to speak; they know no more than what they hear or are shown, and they often repeat it. If the Lord wants me to say something new, His Majesty will provide. Or, He will be pleased to make me remember what I have said at other times, for I would be happy even with this. My memory is so poor that I would be glad if I could repeat, in case they've been lost, some of the things which I was told were well said. If the Lord doesn't make me remember, I will gain just by tiring myself and getting a worse headache for the sake of obedience—even if no one draws any benefit from what I say.[28]

---

27. *The Interior Castle*, Prologue:1.
28. *The Interior Castle*, Prologue:2.

And so I'm beginning to comply today, the feast
of the most Blessed Trinity, in the year 1577, in
this Carmelite monastery of St. Joseph in Toledo
where I am at present. In all that I say I submit
to the opinion of the ones who ordered me to
write, for they are persons of great learning. If I
should say something that isn't in conformity with
what the holy Roman Catholic Church holds, it
will be through ignorance and not through malice.
This can be held as certain, and also that through
the goodness of God I always am, and will be,
and have been subject to her. May He be always
blessed and glorified, amen.[29]

The one who ordered me to write told me that
the nuns in these monasteries of our Lady of Mt.
Carmel need someone to answer their questions
about prayer and that he thought they would better
understand the language used between women,
and that because of the love they bore me they
would pay more attention to what I would tell
them. I thus understand that it was important
for me to manage to say something. So, I shall
be speaking to them while I write; it's nonsense
to think that what I say could matter to other
persons. Our Lord will be granting me favor
enough if some of these nuns benefit by praising
Him a little more. His Majesty well knows that
I don't aim after anything else. And it should be
clear that if I manage to say something well the
Sisters will understand that this does not come
from me since there would be no foundation for
it, unless the Lord gave it to me; otherwise they
would have as little intelligence as I, little ability for
such things.[30]

As in the other prologues, she affirms that she is
writing in obedience to the order of a superior. Then
she makes clear to the readers that in this book she will

29. *The Interior Castle,* Prologue:3.
30. *The Interior Castle,* Prologue: 4.

make the effort not only to remember the things that happened deep down between her soul and God, but also try to remember the words that she used in the *Book of Her Life* so that she can say many things that she wants to say, since they are "some of the things which I was told were well said." But it is necessary to write them again "in case they've been lost." She knew that with the Inquisition the writings could be "lost."

Although she makes clear that she is writing for her sisters, her "daughters", she adds: "It's nonsense to think that what I say could matter to other persons." This was a phrase that she frequently used in her letters: counting on her correspondent's intelligence, she would write the opposite of what she knew and thought. In conclusion, even if *The Interior Castle* – like her other works, *The Book of Her Life, Way of Perfection* and *The Foundations* – were apparently conceived for a circle of readers as carefully chosen as those her first works were addressed to, in reality this is the Teresian book that is addressed most explicitly to an unlimited public. It is a book that is intended not only for the Teresian Carmelites, for contemplatives and mystics, but for everyone, either because of the human element that it contains or because of the emphasis on the supernatural element that underlies every Christian life.

Teresa of Jesus was fully conscious of the universal value of her spiritual writings. She knew that *The Book of Her Life* had already been read enthusiastically and put to use by others, both the learned (letrados) and to those fully devoted to the spirit. The *Way of Perfection* was already circulating in manuscript form among sisters eager to know what made up this interior experience, this friendship with God, in the name of whom Teresa of Jesus had called on them to lock themselves away in a strictly enclosed convent. And in the spring of 1577, the Carthusian monk Hernando de Pantoja had asked her for a copy of her second book. And she knew that the same thing would happen with the book she was now writing. She felt that her books would be read and appreciated after her death.

Once the Prologue was completed, she began by
pretending that she had invented the idea of viewing the
soul as a castle with seven mansions on the very day that
she began to write:

> Today while beseeching our Lord to speak for
> me because I wasn't able to think of anything
> to say nor did I know how to begin to carry out
> this obedience, there came to my mind what I
> shall now speak about, that which will provide us
> with a basis to begin with. It is that we consider
> our soul to be like a castle made entirely out of a
> diamond or of very clear crystal, in which there
> are many rooms, just as in heaven there are many
> dwelling places. For in reflecting upon it carefully,
> Sisters, we realize that the soul of the just person
> is nothing else but a paradise where the Lord says
> He finds His delight. So then, what do you think
> that abode will be like where a King so powerful,
> so wise, so pure, so full of all good things takes
> His delight? I don't find anything comparable to
> the magnificent beauty of a soul and its marvelous
> capacity. Indeed, our intellects, however keen,
> can hardly comprehend it, just as they cannot
> comprehend God; but He Himself says that He
> created us in His own image and likeness. Well
> if this is true, as it is, there is no reason to tire
> ourselves in trying to comprehend the beauty of
> this castle. Since this castle is a creature and the
> difference, therefore, between it and God is the
> same as that between the Creator and His creature,
> His Majesty in saying that the soul is made in His
> own image makes it almost impossible for us to
> understand the sublime dignity and beauty of the
> soul.[31]

Thus, she begins the description of this voyage

---

31. *The Interior Castle, First Dwelling Place,* chapter I:1.

within the castle of the soul: the spiritual progression. The journey that makes up the framework of *The Interior Castle* envisages the spiritual progression as a development in seven stages or Dwelling Places.

The more the soul becomes internalized, i.e. the more it penetrates into the deepest center of itself, the closer it comes to the main Dwelling Place, "where the very secret exchanges between God and the soul take place."[32] She says, "You mustn't think of these dwelling places in such a way that each one would follow in file after the other; but turn your eyes toward the center, which is the room or royal chamber where the King stays."[33] Hence, the closer it draws to God, the more it becomes one with Him and benefits from the light of the divine sun.

In this progression, Teresa distinguishes between two phases, each phase joining together several Dwelling Places. The first phase contains three dwelling places (the First to the Third). In these first dwelling places, there is a recapitulation of the ascetic introduction. The second phase contains four dwelling places (the Fourth to Seventh). In these latter dwelling places, the mystical life will be expounded in greater detail.

In the first phase, God gives what Teresa calls "general grace" and in the second "particular grace," using the terminology found in the *Book of Her Life*.[34] God's general grace is the ordinary assistance provided by grace. Under this regime, the soul maintains the initiative in the spiritual life and a certain independence. It is rather as if God walks side by side with the soul, as it were, assisting it in its operations.

In the second period, God takes the direct initiative to assure the intervention of the gifts of the Holy Spirit. He intervenes in a more and more affirmative way through particular grace until the divine actions are

---

32. *The Interior Castle, First Dwelling Place,* chapter I:3.
33. *The Interior Castle, First Dwelling Place,* chapter I I:8.
34. *Book of Her Life,* Chapter XIV: 6.

truly preponderant. That is to say that the soul loses
the primary place in the organization of its spiritual
life that it had before. Its essential activity will be one
of collaborating with the work of the grace within it.
What had already been taught in the *Book of Her Life*
will appear again more clearly in *The Interior Castle*.
In the later work one sees with new clarity how the
soul, having arrived at the summit of perfection and
totally docile before the movements of the Spirit, can
collaborate perfectly in the design of God's love.

These explanations enable us to understand that
the true spiritual life (in other words, the mystical
life) begins with the second step, i.e. with the Fourth
Dwelling Place. This does not mean that there was
no spiritual life before. However, St. Teresa – like St.
John of the Cross elsewhere - considers the way of
perfection, the march toward sainthood, truly begins in
these four dwelling places and finds its flowering in the
spiritual marriage of the Seventh Dwelling Place.

In describing this itinerary, Teresa provides us with
her concept of the Christian life. The thesis that she
defends in her book of the dwelling places is that the
urgency of mercy for the world commits us to seek
sainthood above all else through an intimate relationship
of friendship with Christ, i.e. though prayer. It is in
this perspective, which had not heretofore been made
specific, that we should read *The Interior Castle* and allow
ourselves to be challenged by it even today. In elevating
St. Teresa to mystical union, the Lord would make of
her an instrument for revealing the work of divine
mercy. She undertakes to describe her experience of
God's mercy so that the greatest number of people can
also experience it.

> It could be that our Lord ordained that they
> command me to write so that we might forget our
> little earthly joys because we will have our eyes set

on the reward and see how immeasurable is His
mercy—since He desires to commune with and
reveal Himself to some worms—and because we
will have these eyes set also on His greatness, and
thus run along enkindled in His love.[35]

In this very compact phrase St. Teresa clearly
expresses her intention. By revealing what God has
done for her, she hopes that the reader will experience
in turn the Lord's merciful love. Unfortunately, the
centuries that have followed St. Teresa have tended to
orient the spiritual life in the direction of a voluntarist
asceticism rather than in the light of the initiative of
divine mercy as revealed in the Scriptures.

Despite the teachings of St. Teresa and St. John of the
Cross (he is also focused entirely on grace), the discalced
Carmelites, influenced by the dominant currents of
the post-Tridentine church, quickly set out on that
path. Henceforward they represented St. Teresa as an
exceptional, out-of-the-ordinary woman, a member of
an elite, in the same way as St. John of the Cross, who is
described as an austere ascetic, lacking in humanity.

These portraits distort reality. These two saints are the
fruit of divine mercy, which, while raising the human
being from misery and deifying such a one by grace, fills
the person with humanity through the example of Jesus
Christ.

St. Teresa, however, was fully persuaded that all of the
mystical favors that she was granted were only a mercy
shown to her so that she could show it better to the rest
of humankind. She is the instrument chosen by God's
mercy for the purpose of being made known to others:
"He grants us a great favor in having communicated
these things to a person through whom we can know
about them. Thus the more we know about His

---

35. *The Interior Castle, Fifth Dwelling Place*, Chapter IV:10.

communication to creatures the more we will praise His grandeur…"[36]

She wants her writings to be a nourishment to strengthen the weak: "These latter will be delighted and awakened through these favors to a greater love of Him who grants so many gifts and whose power and majesty is so great."[37]

For Teresa, to exercise mercy is essentially to reveal to one's neighbor the path by which he or she can experience God's mercy and thus truly know it. It is only in the personal encounter with Christ – in the communication of love – that the human being fully receives the revelation of divine mercy. The written word cannot be a substitute. Teresa has written her books with the sole aim of leading her readers to open themselves to divine mercy. Teresa is acting as a mystagogue; she is "The Mother of Spirituality", she who gives birth to the life of the spirit.

IV. The Text of *The Interior Castle*

1) *The Seven Dwelling Places and the Three Ways of Perfection*

Given the parallel established by the saint between the various kinds of prayer and the degrees of perfection, a good way of finding our way around the Interior Castle will be to determine the relationship that exists between the seven series of dwelling places described by the saint and the three ways of perfection, as these are commonly distinguished by the spiritual tradition.

Following the view of Father Balthazar of St. Catherine, the eminent Carmelite commentator on *The Interior Castle*, we will assign the first three Dwelling Places to the purgative way, the way of those who are

---

36. *The Interior Castle, Seventh Dwelling Place*, Chapter I:1.
37. *The Interior Castle, First Dwelling Place*, Chapter I:4.

beginners. The Fourth Dwelling Place corresponds to the illuminative way, the way of those who are in a state of progress, while the last Dwelling Places, the fifth, sixth and seventh, pertain to the unitive way, the way of those who are perfect. This last point appears clear since St. Teresa herself affirms, with regard to the Fifth Dwelling Place, that the soul can enter there by perfect conformity of its will to the will of God.[38]

We know that, for the saint, such conformity constitutes moral perfection. Thus, the Fifth Dwelling Place pertains to those who are perfect. However, the first three Dwelling Places consider the soul from the moment when it enters into the spiritual life, leading it to a state in which it is rooted in the fear of God, to the point where it can focus all its concerns on spiritual progress. The mystical theologians generally regard this position as the indication of the passage to the illuminative way. Thus, the illuminative way, or the way of those who are in a state of progress, begins after the Third Dwelling Place and the Fourth Dwelling Place is properly attributed to that period in the spiritual life.

2) The Three First Dwelling Places on the Spiritual Journey

St. Teresa does not dwell long on the first Dwelling Places, i.e. the way of those who are beginners. In this new book, *The Interior Castle*, it is her intention to deal specifically with the mystical graces and these are not yet to be found in the first three Dwelling Places. Seeking merely to complete our doctrinal summary with the aid of her mystical teaching, we will therefore limit ourselves to gathering from these first three Dwelling Places those things that enable us to comprehend the structure of the book as a whole. This is why we will first describe the spiritual journey found in *The Interior Castle*.

---

38. *The Interior Castle, Fifth Dwelling Place*, Chapters III, IV and V.

The figurative progression that constitutes the framework of *The Interior Castle* envisages the spiritual journey as a growth in seven steps, or Dwelling Places. In order to better penetrate the symbolic language, let us hear Teresa speak of the founding intuition that lay at the origin of this work. This intuition was given to her in the vision of a soul in a state of grace on the eve of the day of the Trinity, June 2, 1577. It is in this way that she receives from God the fundamental idea, the structure of work in the form of an image. She then immediately sets to work on the day of the feast:

> Today while beseeching our Lord to speak for me because I wasn't able to think of anything to say nor did I know how to begin to carry out this obedience, there came to my mind what I shall now speak about, that which will provide us with a basis to begin with. It is that we consider our soul to be like a castle made entirely out of a diamond or of very clear crystal, in which there are many rooms, just as in heaven there are many dwelling places … some up above, others down below, others to the sides; and in the center and middle is the main dwelling place where the very secret exchanges between God and the soul take place.[39]

The more the soul turns inward, i.e. the more it penetrates into the deepest center of itself, the closer it approaches to the principal dwelling place (the Seventh Dwelling place, where "the King (the Holy Trinity) stays:"

> You mustn't think of these dwelling places in such a way that each one would follow in file after the other; but turn your eyes toward the center, which is the room or royal chamber where the King stays.[40]

Now, the nearer the soul comes to God, the more it

39. *The Interior Castle, Fifth Dwelling Place*, Chapter I:1 and 3.
40. *The Interior Castle, Fifth Dwelling Place*, Chapter II:8.

is unified with Him and benefits from the light of the divine sun:

> Through some secret aspirations the soul
> understands clearly that it is God who gives life
> to our soul. These aspirations come very, very
> often in such a living way that they can in no way
> be doubted ... For just as a great gush of water
> could not reach us if it didn't have a source, as I
> have said, so it is understood clearly that there is
> Someone in the interior depths who shoots these
> arrows and gives life to this life, and that there
> is a Sun in the interior of the soul from which a
> brilliant light proceeds and is sent to the faculties.[41]

3) The Seven Dwelling Places of the Interior Castle and the Seven Degrees of Prayer

In *The Interior Castle* St. Teresa defines the gradations of the way of prayer. The seven Dwelling Places correspond to the same number of degrees of prayer. The first three Dwelling Places correspond to the elementary and ascetic forms of prayer: meditative stammerings that can hardly be heard inside (the First Dwelling Place), meditation and knowledge of oneself (the Second Dwelling Place) and simplified prayer (the Third Dwelling Place).

Teresa does not insist (as she does in the *Way of Perfection*) on the importance of the step of "contemplative prayer," which lays the way for mystical prayer, since this withdrawal into contemplation is precisely the object of the entire book through the symbolism of the Interior Castle.

A transition step follows, leading to the entrance into contemplation. This is an "infused contemplation" (recogimiento infuso), different from the "prayer of quiet," already addressed in the autobiography (chapter

---

41. *The Interior Castle, Fifth Dwelling Place*, Chapter II: 6.

XIV) and in the *Way of Perfection* (chapter XXXI). So
much for the Fourth Dwelling Place.

In the end a third and vast state of union is
established: initial union (the Fifth Dwelling Place),
strong ecstatic experiences (the Sixth Dwelling place)
(here is where Teresa places a whole gamut of mystical
phenomena, such as interior speech, ecstasy, visions,
wounds of love and so on), and contemplative prayer,
perfect in the state of union (the Seventh Dwelling
Place).

In *The Interior Castle* the beginning of the spiritual life
is made dependent on the capacity of the person to be
the image and abode of God (chapter I:1). It develops
in accordance with the capacity for relationship and
configuration with Christ (Fifth Dwelling Place, chapters
I-III) and culminates in the mysterious union with God
(Seventh Dwelling Place).

The entire process is divided into seven steps or
Dwelling Places, but powerful symbols emphasize
three moments. The symbol of the Interior Castle
states that the human person is the abode of God, but
an abode open to a vast range of potentialities. The
second symbol (the metamorphosis of the silkworm
into the butterfly) shows that the entire Christian life is
a process of configuration and union with Christ (Fifth
Dwelling Place). Finally, the nuptial symbol, here fully
developed, accentuates the truth that the spiritual life
of the Christian does not lie so much in the person's
ethical unfurling as in the full interpersonal communion
of God and the human being (Fifth, Sixth and Seventh
Dwelling Places).

Finally, Teresa describes sainthood through four
complementary realities (Seventh Dwelling Place): the
residence of the Trinity within the soul, which is the
achievement of St. John the Baptist's promise (chapters

XIV and XXIII and Seventh Dwelling Place, chapter I), union with Christ through the spiritual marriage (Seventh Dwelling Place, chapter II), the human fullness of the new creature (Seventh Dwelling Place, chapter III) and the complete configuration with Christ in the service of humanity and the Church (Seventh Dwelling Place, chapter IV).

V. First and Second Dwelling Places: Entry Into the Spiritual Life

1) First Dwelling Place: "The Door of Entry Into This Castle is Prayer."

St. Teresa begins her description of the journey into the castle of the soul by returning to a theme that she had already developed in the *Way of Perfection*, when she had said to the sisters of St. Joseph of Avila, "within us lies something incomparably more precious than what we see outside ourselves," and that they should imagine that they were "hollow inside." This is the theme of the soul being a depth to be explored, where one can enter into a knowledge of oneself which – since the soul is made in the image and likeness of God – is also the desire to know Him, the foundation of the love of Him and for Him. And the first step should be the search for an identity, for knowing "who" you are in relation to God.

> It is a shame and unfortunate that through our own fault we don't understand ourselves or know who we are. Wouldn't it show great ignorance … if someone when asked who he was didn't know, and didn't know his father or mother or from what country he came? Well now, if this would be so extremely stupid, we are incomparably more so when we do not strive to know who we are, but limit ourselves to considering only roughly these bodies. Because we have heard and because faith

tells us so, we know we have souls. But we seldom consider the precious things that can be found in this soul, or who dwells within it, or its high value. Consequently, little effort is made to preserve its beauty.[42]

For in reflecting upon it carefully, Sisters, we realize that the soul of the just person is nothing else but a paradise where the Lord says He finds His delight. So then, what do you think that abode will be like where a King so powerful, so wise, so pure, so full of all good things takes His delight? I don't find anything comparable to the magnificent beauty of a soul and its marvelous capacity. Indeed, our intellects, however keen, can hardly comprehend it, just as they cannot comprehend God; but He Himself says that He created us in His own image and likeness.

Well if this is true, as it is, there is no reason to tire ourselves in trying to comprehend the beauty of this castle. Since this castle is a creature and the difference, therefore, between it and God is the same as that between the Creator and His creature, His Majesty in saying that the soul is made in His own image makes it impossible for us to understand the sublime dignity and beauty of the soul. [43]

It should be noted that, side by side with the ascetic current of knowledge of oneself based on the psychological analysis and personal effort developed principally by St. Ignatius in his Spiritual Exercises, there also exists a mystical current, arising in particular from St. Teresa and St. John of the Cross, which is directed to self-knowledge through the revelatory presence of God in ourselves. In a surprising way the Christian mystics, although they seem to be turned totally toward

---

42. *The Interior Castle, First Dwelling Place*, Chapter I: 2.
43. *The Interior Castle, First Dwelling Place*, Chapter I: 1.

God, very intensely stress the need for self-knowledge, to the point of putting it on the same footing as the knowledge of God, as St. Augustine did before them. St. Augustine even places the knowledge of self on the same footing as the knowledge of God: "*Noverim me, noverim te*" (Let me know myself, let me know you). "*Deum et animam scire cupio*" (I want to know God and the soul).[44] God and the human being are the two poles of one and the same experience. The actualization of this fundamental relationship between the person and God is prayer, which is the entry into the spiritual life:

> Insofar as I can understand the door of entry to this castle is prayer and reflection. I don't mean to refer to mental more than vocal prayer, for since vocal prayer is prayer it must be accompanied by reflection. A prayer in which a person is not aware of whom he is speaking to, what he is asking, who it is who is asking and of whom, I do not call prayer however much the lips move.[45]

Thus, the thing that permits us to penetrate into the castle of the soul, i.e. into the dimension of interiority proper to the spiritual life, is the prayer that Teresa characterizes as the "door of entry to this castle."[46] Those who have not understood this are like the crippled or the paralyzed, who have limbs to act and move, but are incapable of using them:

> Thus there are souls so ill and so accustomed to being involved in external matters that there is no remedy, not does it seem they can enter within themselves. They are now so used to dealing always with the insects and vermin that are in the wall surrounding the castle that they have become almost like them. And though they have so rich a nature and the power to converse with none

---

44. St. Augustin, *Works, Soliloquies* II, 1; I, 7.
45. *The Interior Castle, First Dwelling Place*, Chapter I: 7.
46. *The Interior Castle, First Dwelling Place*, Chapter I: 7.

other than God, there is no remedy. If these souls
do not strive to understand and cure their great
misery, they will be changed into statues of salt,
unable to turn their heads to look at themselves,
just as Lot's wife was changed for having turned
her head.[47]

These souls are encamped outside of themselves, in
the moats of the castle, a very dangerous place crawling
with "the insects and vermin," with everything that leads
to sin.

This situation can only be precarious, since "in the
midst of such poisonous creatures one cannot help but
be bitten at one time or another," Teresa warns.[48]

To penetrate into the castle, i.e. to begin to live truly
the life of grace, it is necessary to avoid mortal sin,
for this rules out any possibility of any "commerce"
with God.[49] However, though they enter with good
intentions,[50] they also enter with all of their attachments,
their faults, their bad tendencies: the "many reptiles." [51]
Thus they "are easily conquered, even though they may
go about with desires not to offend God and though
they do perform good works."[52]

Even though they may be "in a bad state," they are
"so absorbed with its possessions, honor, or business
affairs" that their way of access to God becomes
extremely difficult for them. These obstacles and
attachments risk at all times leading them again into
sin. "In the midst of such poisonous creatures one
cannot help but be bitten at one time or another."[53]
And this may happen all the more easily since in this

47. *The Interior Castle, First Dwelling Place*, Chapter I: 6.
48. *The Interior Castle, First Dwelling Place*, Chapter II:14.
49. *The Interior Castle, First Dwelling Place*, Chapter I:8.
50. *The Interior Castle, First Dwelling Place*, Chapter II:12.
51. *The Interior Castle, First Dwelling Place*, Chapter I: 8.
52. *The Interior Castle, First Dwelling Place*, Chapter II:12.
53. *The Interior Castle, First Dwelling Place*, Chapter II:14.

First Dwelling Place the life of prayer is very weak and intermittent. It may be compared to those breaths of air that a swimmer must take from time to time to avoid asphyxia. It is in this way that these souls sometimes succeed in tearing themselves away from their usual earthly concerns in order to entrust themselves "once in a while" to our Lord.[54] However, it is in this dialogue with the Lord that the key to the progression, to the dynamic structure of the way of prayer is found. This is why Teresa presses us to embark resolutely on the road of detachment and commerce with God. It is not enough to have already penetrated into the First Dwelling Place of the castle to have the guarantee of staying there. To do that, or more precisely to progress, spiritual asceticism is essential. Otherwise, the bites of venomous beasts risk pushing the soul all the way back to the castle moat.[55] As always in Teresa's spirituality, the progress of the soul will depend on progress in prayer. And this is the case with those who attain the Second Dwelling Place.

2) The Second Dwelling Place

A) A More Determined Commitment to Prayer

The souls that reach the Second Dwelling Place are not satisfied with simply commending themselves to God "every now and then," but, understanding better the importance of prayer, they have begun to devote themselves to it. They have become more sensitive to the multiple appeals of the Lord, which went practically unheard in the First Dwelling Place.

> So these persons are able to hear the Lord when he calls. Since they are getting close to where His Majesty dwells, He is a very good neighbor. His mercy and goodness are so bountiful; whereas

---

54. *The Interior Castle, First Dwelling Place*, Chapter I:8.
55. *The Interior Castle, First Dwelling Place*, Chapter II:14.

we are occupied in our pastimes, business affairs,
pleasures, and worldly buying and selling, and still
falling into sin and rising again. These beasts are
so poisonous and their presence so dangerous
and noisy that it would be a wonder if we kept
from stumbling and falling over them. Yet this
Lord desires intensely that we love Him and seek
His company, so much so that from time to time
He calls us to draw near Him. And His voice
is so sweet the poor soul dissolves at not doing
immediately what He commands… Thus, as I say,
hearing His voice is a greater trial than not hearing
it.[56]

Regarding these "appeals and calls" of God, Teresa
states:

But they come through words spoken by other
good people, or through sermons, or through what
is read in good books, or through many things
that are heard and by which God calls, or through
illnesses and trials, or also through a truth that He
teaches during the brief moments we spend in
prayer; however lukewarm these moments may be,
God esteems them highly.[57]

We already know from Teresa's early teachings at what
point prayer is the remedy suited to healing moral and
spiritual weakness. Her actual abandonment of prayer
for a year (or a little more) had distanced her from the
source of any spiritual progress.[58] Teresa will draw from
this bitter experience the important lesson that the more
one feels oneself to be a sinner, they more one should
deliver oneself to prayer and not give it up.[59]

For Teresa prayer is a remedy for moral weakness if
it is experienced in humility and repentance, as well as

56. *The Interior Castle, Second Dwelling Place*, Chapter I:2.
57. *The Interior Castle, Second Dwelling Place*, Chapter I:3.
58. *Book of Her Life,* Chapter VII:11 and Chapter XIX:4.
59. *Book of Her Life,* Chapter VIII:4-5, 6-8; Chapter XV:3 ; Chapter XIX:4,
11 and 12.

in flight from dangerous situations. After having first denied it, Teresa recognized that a soul, even in a state of mortal sin ("in a bad state"), has the possibility of receiving God's mercy, with the gift of justification, of supernatural contemplation. This is precisely in order to permit it to abandon its habit of sin.

Let us also recall the very precious warning given in the *Book of Her Life*:

> It is that in spite of any wrong they who practice prayer do, they must not abandon prayer since it is the means by which they can remedy the situation; and to remedy it without prayer would be much more difficult.[60]

It is thus of great importance for the soul to "understand the great good God does for a soul that willingly disposes itself for the practice of prayer, even though it is not disposed as is necessary," since "if the soul perseveres in prayer, in the midst of the sins, temptations, and failures of a thousand kinds that the devil places in its path ... I hold as certain, the Lord will draw it forth to the harbor of salvation ..."[61]

This exhortation to fidelity in prayer, so as to become greater in virtue, is a particularly useful encouragement in these very laborious beginnings of the Second Dwelling Place.

Thus, the essential effort in this step will consist of cultivating, no matter what the cost, "intimate sharing between friends" with the Lord. And in fact the cost is high for the person who seeks to commit himself to it.

The cross is well represented in the first plunge into the life of prayer, as Teresa has already indicated in the first way of watering the garden, i.e. "you may draw

---

60. *Book of Her Life,* Chapter VIII:5.
61. *Book of Her Life,* Chapter VIII:4.

water from a well (which is for us a lot of work)."[62] And, as she explains, by setting out on the road of prayer, one assumes the "determination" (a quite characteristic word in Teresa's vocabulary) not to stop halfway, but "to reach the summit of perfection,"[63] which is the clearly stated objective.

This assumes, from the beginning, embracing of the cross with constant "determination", by supporting all the aridities, all the distastes that are the lot of the life of prayer. In fact, Teresa is saying that we do not resort to prayer to find there consolations and emotional sentiments, but to become truly the "servant of love."[64] In no case can authentic prayer nourish an egocentric mentality. On the contrary, it is in itself the source of the spirit of service.

Thus, one can say that the cross is the walking staff that will support the soul in its decision to strive for union of its will with that of the Lord:

> The whole aim of anyone who is beginning prayer
> … should be that he work and prepare himself
> with determination and every possible effort to
> bring his will into conformity with God's will…
> Be certain that, as I shall say later, the greatest
> perfection attainable along the spiritual path lies in
> this conformity.[65]

To learn to know God by looking at him, to find in this look of faith the strength necessary to act in his service: this is the purpose of prayer.[66].

B) To Learn to Know God in Order to Act in His Service

In fact, the internal rhythm of the life of prayer consists in finding God in faith in order to testify to

---

62. *Book of Her Life,* Chapter XI:7.
63. *Book of Her Life,* Chapter XI:4.
64. *Book of Her Life,* Chapter XI:1.
65. *The Interior Castle, Second Dwelling Place*, Chapter I:8.
66. *The Interior Castle, Second Dwelling Place*, Chapter I:11.

the divine love among people. If it is clear that in *The Interior Castle* the concern for remaining faithful to God mobilizes the most essential forces of the soul and prevails over the concern for outward testimony, it is no less true that, from this moment forward, the germ of apostolic zeal takes root in it. This zeal will develop gradually to the extent of the soul's perseverance in prayer, through all spiritual struggles. This is indeed Teresa's conviction:

> Well, if we never look at Him or reflect on what we owe Him and the death he suffered for us, I don't know how we'll be able to know Him or do works in His service.[67]

As the apostle St. James did, Teresa teaches that a faith worthy of the name should lead to works:

> And what value can faith have without works and without joining them to the merits of Jesus Christ, our Good?[68]

The personal misery discovered in prayer must not inhibit the zeal for God. On the contrary, it should strengthen it, in view of the works to be done, for when we turn toward God, "… our intellects and wills, dealing in turn now with self now with God, become nobler and better prepared for every good."[69]

All the more so since, in this Second Dwelling Place, "if the devil, especially, realizes that it has all it needs in temperament and habits to advance far, he will gather all hell together to make the soul go back outside."[70]

Only a determined involvement in Christ's cross can vanquish it.[71]

This dwelling place then is truly the Dwelling Place

67. *The Interior Castle, Second Dwelling Place,* Chapter I:11.
68. *The Interior Castle, Second Dwelling Place,* Chapter I:11.
69. *The Interior Castle, First Dwelling Place,* Chapter II:1.
70. *The Interior Castle, Second Dwelling Place,* Chapter I:5.
71. *The Interior Castle, Second Dwelling Place,* Chapter I:6.

of struggle and perseverance or of perseverance in the struggle.

In conclusion, I will endeavor to summarize briefly the ideas that are expressed in these first two dwelling places and to point out their dynamic spiritual structure.

We enter then the first Dwelling Place of the Interior Castle, the foundation of which is our soul, considered as a castle made of a single perfectly clear diamond or crystal, in which there are, as in heaven, many dwelling places[72] and in which God Himself lives.

We are vaguely aware, St. Teresa says, that we have a soul because we have heard it talked about and this is what faith teaches us. But we rarely reflect on the riches that this soul may enclose, of the Host that resides there and on its inestimable value. All our attention is focused on the wall that surrounds this castle, our perishable body. Our souls are crippled, St. Teresa adds, and will be changed into statues of salt because they are "unable to turn their heads to look at themselves." It is in these familiar, almost popular terms that the Castilian mystic translates the famous "nosce te ipsum" ("Know thyself"). The idea of withdrawal into contemplation, of introspection, so hard to make the people understand, is so admirably expressed, and in the language of the people: "Turn their heads to look at themselves" (Volver la cabeza hacia sí). But there would be a danger of shutting oneself in and becoming lost in this contemplation of the self. St. Teresa perceives this and opposed good sense as a counterbalance. After having described this interior castle, consisting of a number of rooms arranged around the central room where the King dwells, like so much skine around the fruit, she adds:

> Don't force it to stay a long time in one room

---

72. John 14:2.

alone. Oh, but if it is in the room of self-
knowledge!... But let's remember that the bee
doesn't fail to leave the beehive and fly about
gathering nectar from the flowers. So it is with the
soul in the room of self-knowledge; let it believe
me and fly sometimes to ponder the grandeur
and majesty of its God. Here it will discover its
lowliness better than by thinking of itself.

Moreover, in this first Dwelling House, the souls,
already blinded by the concerns of this world and
caught up in its whirlwind, resemble someone who has
his eyes full of dust and cannot enjoy the brightness
of the sun. It is as Plotin says: "Someone who sees has
to make himself like the thing seen before starting to
contemplate it." To contemplate and to see the things
of the heavens, we must first remove the dirt from our
eyes.

In the Second Dwelling Place, we draw nearer to
God, to that God who is a good neighbor. This good
Teacher attaches such a high price to our love and our
efforts that He never ceases to call out to us and invite
us to approach Him. Having such a good Host, whose
mercy and generosity are so great, the soul no longer
seeks peace and goodness in other dwelling places.
It quits imitating the erratic behavior of the prodigal
son and, like him, relishing the food of swine. Can we
find more vivid expressions to make us understand the
theological ideas of the presence of God within us, of
His generous paternal love for us, the cause of all peace
and all goodness?

However, St. Teresa does not lose sight of her starting
point. She says that "it is foolish to think that we will
enter heaven without entering into ourselves." But if
we have to enter into ourselves, it just isn't in order to
go there and do nothing. On the contrary, it is in order
to know ourselves, to discover our misery and God's

goodness, to beg for His mercy and to struggle against ourselves, for we are our most mortal enemies, as we are those of God. For all of our perfection consists in renouncing our own will in order to shape it to that of God. The more perfect this conformity is, the more we receive from the Lord, the more we advance on the spiritual path. And, St. Teresa continues shrewdly, "Don't think that in what concerns perfection there is more mystery or things unknown or still to be understood", thus dismissing in a single phrase the complicated discourses, the rantings and fashions in which those who pretend to live a spiritual life but do not do so become lost. Without God's assistance, everything is dark, everything is impossible. With it, everything is bright, everything is easy. It is only necessary to conform oneself to the divine will and persevere in that.

VI. The Third Dwelling Place: The Culmination of the Ascetic Dwelling Places or the Triumph of Reasonable Activity

We have now come to the Third Dwelling Place. It is an important step in the conquest of interiority. It also marks an advance in obedience to God. The first verse of Psalm 112, which is placed at the beginning of the first chapter, seems to summarize in itself the state of the soul that has reached this point: "How blessed is anyone who fears Yahweh…" Thus, the Third Dwelling Place is for those who fear the Lord and who, for a good reason, are called blessed. For if they do not go back, they are, so far as we can judge, on a sure path to salvation. Henceforward, the soul desires to place its entire existence under the watchful eye of God, organizing it humanly and spiritually to this end. This is the quiet domination of a reasonable activity: embracing both the life of prayer and apostolic commitment. This is the triumph of wise organization:

> [The souls] long not to offend His Majesty, even guarding themselves against venial sins; they are fond of doing penance and setting aside periods for withdrawal into contemplation; they spend their time well, practicing works of charity toward their neighbors; and are very balanced in their speech and dress and in the governing of their households—those who have them.[73]

Teresa's verdict as to the value of this state is clearly positive:

> For the Lord has done them no small favor, but a very great one.[74]

She obviously does not spare her admiration:

> Certainly, this is a state to be desired ... for such a desired way is an excellent way to prepare oneself so that every favor may be granted.[75]

Nevertheless, a careful reading of all the words gradually reveals a sort of reserve, even at some moments a sharp, if measured, irony. As a whole, in the two chapters that deal with the Third Dwelling House, sincere admiration and lucid criticism are mixed together and rub against each other until finally a decisive light is brought forth. It is more instructive to seek the reason for Teresa's reserve than to dwell on the sincerity of her compliments, which in any case quickly give way to an appeal to commit oneself in the most radical way possible.

The presumptuous, those who, like the Pharisee of the Gospel, believe that they are superior to others, would do well, in order to set aside any temptation for spiritual pride, to read what St. Teresa says. Only

---

73. *The Interior Castle, Third Dwelling Place*, Chapter I:5.
74. *The Interior Castle, Third Dwelling Place*, Chapter I:5.
75. *Ibid.*

the souls who are intent on avoiding even venial sins, who exert themselves in works of charity toward their neighbor, who love penitence and have their hours of withdrawal into contemplation, can enter into this Third Dwelling House.

The episode in the Gospel of the rich young man (Matthew 19: 16-22) referred to in the text enables her to understand and characterize the behavior of the soul in this period. On the basis of the rich young man's reaction to Jesus' invitation to follow him after selling all he possesses and giving it to the poor, Teresa remarks to her daughters (and through them to all of us) that, in order to actually attain perfection, it is not enough to proclaim one's desire for it. "......there is need of still more in order that the soul possess the Lord completely ..." [76]

So what do they lack?

The same thing as Jesus' interlocutor, the young rich man. That is, to give up one's possessions in order to follow Christ! There is a knot that one must strive to untie. For the flaw in these souls is to try to accommodate God and themselves at the same time – God and their attachment to the world. In other words, their imperfection consists in relying more on their own person and on the maxims of the world than on God. This attitude engenders in them an esteem hidden from themselves that prompts them, as it were, to boast to God of their works. All this is not necessarily perfectly obvious, but rather is concealed under a subtle pride, more or less conscious, that is "distilled" in everyday actions. In response, Teresa calls upon them to show humility, selflessness and self-sacrifice:

> Pass on from your little works (pasad adelante de vuestras obrillas). By the mere fact that you are

---

76. *The Interior Castle, Third Dwelling Place*, Chapter I:6.

> Christians you must do all these things and much more.[77]

Moreover, in their works (or even their sufferings), which they tend to emphasize, they content themselves most of the time with a simple human prudence that makes them secretly satisfied with the organization of the Christian life which they have attained, admittedly through their worthy efforts. However, they do not place this good result entirely in the hands of God, to Whom they owe it all. They somehow appropriate it to themselves by wishing to remain the mistresses and principal managers of their spiritual life. Teresa stigmatizes this attitude.

When, in the second chapter, Teresa cites several specific examples to illustrate the behavior of these souls, we feel her irony broaden and her criticism become very clear. She exclaims:

> "They like much their life put at the service of Our Lord…" [78]

This is a way of saying that they prefer to bet on their modest measure of reason than to let the love of Christ carry them beyond their limits. They love their spiritual life more than what gives rise to it. In the final analysis, the major reproach is that they do not love enough, that they do not become "fools for Christ," as St. Paul says (1 Corinthians 4:10), and thus going beyond all human prudence:

> Have no fear that they will kill themselves, for their reason is still very much in control. Love has not yet reached the point of overwhelming reason. But I should like us to use our reason to make ourselves dissatisfied with this way of serving God, always going step by step, for we'll never

---

77. *The Interior Castle, Third Dwelling Place*, Chapter I:6.
78. *The Interior Castle, Third Dwelling Place*, Chapter II:7.

finish this journey.[79]

Divine wisdom actually takes us beyond the human measure. When Wisdom asks us to do so, we must of course respond with acts, with an actual commitment of our whole selves, with what Teresa calls "works" *(obras)*. However, she also makes clear that the value of our commitment does not rest principally on our works, but on the "determination of our wills."

> And don't think He needs our works; He needs the determination of our wills.[80]

Since the only definitive mark of love is the determination of our will, it is not enough to say that we want to follow Jesus. Something more is needed for God to be the absolute master of a soul. The rich young man whom God asked if he wanted to be perfect is the proof. Certain servants of God who have arrived at this condition imagine they have put God under the obligation to repay a debt that is owed to them and they themselves don't owe any more. And St. Teresa answers them, "You owe everything." For the only definitive mark of love is the determination of our will. Hence, these souls that are so well organized and so satisfied with being that way, are they ready to consider themselves a "useless servant," to humbly practice the common virtues, to subject their will to that of God in all things, so that their life will unfold in the conditions chosen by God and not by them? St. Teresa says:

> The penance these souls do is well balanced, like their lives. They desire penance a great deal so as to serve our Lord by it. Nothing of this is wrong, and thus they are very discreet in doing it in a way so as not to harm their health. Have no fear that

---

79. *The Interior Castle, Third Dwelling Place*, Chapter II:7; see *Book of Her Life*, Chapter XIII: 5, where Teresa uses the expression "*paso de gallina*" (chicken step).

80. *The Interior Castle, Third Dwelling Place*, Chapter I:7.

> they will kill themselves, for their reason is still
> very much in control. Love has not yet reached the
> point of overwhelming reason. But I should like
> us to use our reason to make ourselves dissatisfied
> with this way of serving God, always going step by
> step, for we'll never finish this journey.[81]

This amounts to saying that what the Lord expects
from us is not so much a display of internal or external
actions that we are pleased to imagine a priori as being
powerful, but rather a free, loving and – above all –
humble adherence of our will to the divine design of
love. For in the end it is God who produces in us the
fruitfulness of our works. Since God's appeal is without
cost, pure mercy, it is essential to keep in our heart the
necessary sense of this gratuitousness and detachment
with regard to the fruits that spring from it. Awareness
of this reality in faith engenders an attitude of grateful
humility, typical of those who are viscerally convinced,
in the sincere poverty of their heart, that they are only a
"useless servant." Speaking of the destitution necessary
to all spiritual life, Teresa alludes to a passage in the
Gospel of St. Luke:

> There is no doubt that if a person perseveres in
> this nakedness and detachment from all worldly
> things he will reach his goal. But this perseverance
> includes the condition- and note that I am advising
> you of this—that you consider yourselves useless
> servants, as St. Paul or Christ (Luke 17:10), says;
> and believe that you have not put our Lord under
> any obligation to grant you these kinds of favors.[82]

This profound conviction, rooted in the theology
of grace, does not paralyze us for action, bur rather
liberates us, since it places the apostle in his true place
as God's collaborator. Because of this, it prompts the
<u>indispensable</u> disappropriation with regard to our works,

81. *The Interior Castle, Third Dwelling Place*, Chapter II:7.
82. *The Interior Castle, Third Dwelling Place*, Chapter I:8.

which in the final analysis rest only on the divine power. In order to promote this effort at detachment, Teresa points out the precious help provided by obedience.

In developing this point, Teresa is careful to note that obedience does not concern only those men and women who aremembers of religious orders, but also all Christians desirous of progressing spiritually.

> What it seems to me would be highly beneficial for those who through the goodness of the Lord are in this state is that they study diligently how to be prompt in obedience. And even if they are not members of a religious order, it would be a great thing for them to have—as do many persons—someone whom they could consult so as not to do their own will in anything. Doing our own will is usually what harms us. And they shouldn't seek another of their own making; as they say—one who is so circumspect about everything; but seek out someone who is very free from illusion about the things of the world.[83]

Obedience to such a person is a favored means of surpassing one's own will and one's limited views and delivering oneself over to the will of God. This is a means all the more necessary since in the Third Dwelling Place the soul remains fragile and exposed to sin and to turning back.

> Since they are close to the first dwelling places, they could easily return to them. Their fortitude is not founded on solid ground.[84]

Through the practice of obedience, the theological life is purified, permitting the soul to cling more closely, in the darkness, to God's hidden design. In this way, the believer is immersed more and more in God's rhythm. In the final analysis, obedience is worth only as much

---

83. *The Interior Castle, Third Dwelling Place*, Chapter II:12.
84. *Ibid.*

as the gift of oneself to the Lord that underlies it. The sincerity of this gift opens the door to divine action. Hence, it is not the time to turn one's back, like the young man in the gospel did. Rather, "What do you want His Majesty to do? For he must give the reward in conformity with the love we have for Him."

The gift of self is the condition, sine qua non, for receiving God's free gift and thus entering into the mystical life. St. Teresa writes in the *Way of Perfection*:

> Because everything I have advised you about in this book is directed toward the complete gift of ourselves to the Creator, the surrender of our wills to His, and detachment from creatures; ... we are preparing ourselves that we may quickly reach the end of our journey and drink the living water from the fount we mentioned (that is to say contemplation). Unless we give our wills entirely to the Lord so that in everything pertaining to us He might do what conforms with His will, we will never be allowed to drink from this fount.[85]

Such affirmations clearly tie the entry into contemplation with the offering of self made to the Lord. This spirituality of the gift of self was a central point in the teachings that Teresa never ceases to extol to her sisters and through them to all Christians. In order to receive the love that flows from God, to arrive at the summit of perfection, it is necessary to be poor and above all to continue to be poor, while offering ourselves, such as we are, to the mercy of God. This is because we do not give ourselves to God completely and finally, since the divine love cannot pervade us completely and finally: "But it seems to us that we are giving all to God, whereas the truth of the matter is that we are paying God the rent or giving Him the fruits and

---

85. *Way of Perfection*, Chapter XXXII:9.

keeping for ourselves the ownership and the root." [86]

VII. The Fourth Dwelling Place: Step-By-Step Advances of God

The illuminative way opens to us the region where mystical contemplation develops in the soul. There we are present at the birth and progress of a new life that invades the soul and deeply penetrates it, finally transforming it completely and making of it a truly divine life. Teresa adroitly uses a number of comparisons to make the mystery of the deeper supernatural life more understandable. Of these, her favorite is that of water:

> Let's consider, for a better understanding, that we see two founts with two water troughs. (For I don't find anything more appropriate to explain some spiritual experiences than water; and this is because I know little and have no helpful cleverness of mind and am so fond of this element that I have observed it more attentively than other things. In all things that so great and wise a God has created there must be many beneficial secrets, and those who understand them do benefit, although I believe that in each little thing created by God there is more than what is understood, even if it is a little ant.)[87]

Using the idea of water, the saint initiates us into the properties of the prayer of quiet, which is characteristic of the Fourth Dwelling Place. She usually calls these "delight in God" and explains to us how these "delights" are different than the contentments produced by meditation. Let us imagine, she says, that we are in the presence of two fountains that fill two basins with water.

---

86. *Book of Her Life,* Chapter XI:2.
87. *The Interior Castle, Fourth Dwelling Place*, Chapter II:2.

With one the water comes from far away through
many aqueducts and the use of much ingenuity;
with the other the source of the water is right
there, and the trough fills without any noise ... The
water coming from the aqueducts is comparable,
in my opinion, to the consolations I mentioned
that are drawn from meditation. For we obtain
them through thoughts, assisting ourselves, using
creatures to help our meditations, and tiring the
intellect. Since, in the end, the consolation comes
through our own efforts, noise is made when there
has to be some replenishing of the benefits the
consolation causes in the soul.[88] With this other
fount, the water comes from its own source which
is God. And since His Majesty desires to do so—
when He is pleased to grant some supernatural
favor—He produces this delight with the greatest
peace and quiet and sweetness in the very interior
part of ourselves. I don't know from where or
how, nor is that happiness and delight experienced,
as are earthly consolations, in the heart. I mean
there is no similarity at the beginning, for
afterward the delight fills everything; this water
overflows through all the dwelling places and
faculties until reaching the body.[89]

Before long the effect of this heavenly water makes
itself felt in the soul:

It seems that since that heavenly water begins to
rise from this spring I'm mentioning that is deep
within us, it swells and expands our whole interior
being, producing ineffable blessings; nor does the
soul even understand what is given to it there ...
This spiritual delight is not something that can be
imagined, because however, diligent our efforts we
cannot acquire it.[90]

---

88. *The Interior Castle, Fourth Dwelling Place*, Chapter II:3.
89. *The Interior Castle, Fourth Dwelling Place*, Chapter II:4.
90. *The Interior Castle, Fourth Dwelling Place*, Chapter II: 6.

Thus, the mystical life begins through a new free gift of God, who, in response to the attitude of the humble, loving and open availability of the soul, takes hold of it and thus leads it, from detachment to detachment, to the transforming union. It is here, in the Fourth Dwelling Place, that St. Teresa again stresses the importance of humility, disinterestedness and love in order to receive the gift of contemplation:

> After you have done what should be done by those in the previous dwelling places: humility! humility! By this means the Lord allows Himself to be conquered with regard to anything we want from Him. The first sign for seeing whether or not you have humility is that you do not think you deserve these favors and spiritual delights from the Lord or that you will receive them in your lifetime.[91]

Prayer blossoms into contemplation and the apostolate becomes mystical. What was previously based essentially on a natural activity assisted by grace now rests in the first place on an obedience of faith to the Spirit of God. This is the principle. But this principle, once it has been laid down, requires the introduction of some very essential details! In fact, contemplation cannot be perfect in the beginning since it is not continuous. Thus, the practice of prayer must find a fair balance between the supernatural action of God and the activity of the soul that will compensate for the momentary absence of contemplation:

> When through His secret paths it seems we understand that He hears us, then it is good to be silent since He has allowed us to remain near Him; and it will not be wrong to avoid working with the intellect—if we can work with it, I mean. But if we don't yet know whether this King has heard or seen us, we mustn't become fools.[92]

---

91. *The Interior Castle, Fourth Dwelling Place*, Chapter II:9.
92. *The Interior Castle, Fourth Dwelling Place*, Chapter III:5.

In this dwelling place, the divine and the human are very closely interlinked, which sometimes make it a very delicate matter to discern the action of Grace.

In the context of the Fourth Dwelling Place, we speak of a contrasting experience. As it progresses in the soul, grace simultaneously enriches and disrupts. While the enrichment is indisputable, the paradoxical way in which it occurs calls for some explanation, for it will surely have an impact on the way we envisage and experience apostolic engagement.

The emerging experience of contemplation makes the soul unable to meditate as it did before. The intellect ceases to operate because God suspends it. From this point on, it is the Lord who nourishes the soul directly:

> When His Majesty desires the intellect to stop, He occupies it in another way and gives it a light so far above what we can attain that it remains absorbed. Then, without knowing how, the intellect is much better instructed than it was through all the soul's efforts not to make use of it.[93]

The action of God makes itself felt in a new way, not without repercussions on the faculties, which experience in a confused way something of the divine presence and power. It is then that the soul better perceives the need for divine help in prayer, since God makes it understand that "without Him we can do nothing,"[94] that God is the Master of prayer. This new experience of God in contemplation also gives the soul a keener awareness of its weakness in general (which certainly includes awareness of sin in particular). The image of the castle of the soul, a magnificent crystal, illuminated by the very clear brilliance and splendor of the divine Sun, completes the descriptions given in the autobiography and enables us to grasp the interaction between divine

93. *The Interior Castle, Fourth Dwelling Place*, Chapter III:6.
94. *The Interior Castle, Fourth Dwelling Place*, Chapter I:4.

purity and the darkness of sin. The closer we draw
to the light that radiates from the center of the soul,
the more it illuminates the dark corners with their bad
tendencies and their sins.

Benefiting from the supernatural clarity that flows
from contemplation, the knowledge of self goes
far beyond the discoveries of simple psychological
contemplation. Fruit of the gift of knowledge, self-
knowledge illuminates the soul and all creation as to
their intrinsic value by placing them under the light of
God as Truth.

In this first form of supernatural prayer, the soul lives
simultaneously in the divine light and in the darkness
of faith. It feels at the same time the strength of
God and its personal weakness. In the midst of this
contrasting experience, however, one trait emerges, that
of "expansion or dilation of the soul" *(dilatamiento o
ensanchamiento en el alma).*[95] In the three chapters of this
Fourth Dwelling Place, one quotation returns several
times: *"Cum dilatasti cor meum"* (You have dilated my
heart).[96] In this very short extract from Psalm 119[97] Teresa
desires to have us perceive at what point the prayer of
quietude, by expanding the soul's capacity to receive the
divine, opens to it at the same time ever new horizons:

> So it seems is that case with this prayer and many
> other marvels that God grants to the soul, for
> He enables and prepares it so that it can keep
> everything within itself.[98]

"Everything" means all of the immense favors with
which God fills and wants to fill the soul. It is God
himself!

---

95. *The Interior Castle, Fourth Dwelling Place*, Chapter III:9.
96. *The Interior Castle, Fourth Dwelling Place*, Chapter I:5 and 6 ; see also
Chapter III:9.
97. Psalm 119, 32b.
98. *The Interior Castle, Fourth Dwelling Place*, Chapter III:9.

Speaking of the prayer of contemplation in the *Way of Perfection*, Teresa writes:

> So that the soul won't be disturbed in the beginning by seeing that it is too small to have something so great within itself, the Lord doesn't give it this knowledge until He enlarges it little by little and it has the capacity to receive what He will place within (the soul).[99]

Of the fact of the divine presence and its action, she writes:

> … the soul is not as tied down as it was before in things pertaining to the service of God, but has much more freedom.[100]

It is a flowering, a liberation that begins from the viewpoint of both the life of prayer and of the moral life and that of service to God. This is due to the fact that in the prayer of quiet "everything is 'yes'"[101] to the Lord because of the hold (if transitory) that God exercises on the free will.

In order to understand better what this state represents for prayer, it would be necessary to repeat in detail the numerous passages relating the way in which God dilates the soul through sweetness and quietude and thus begins to "give you the Kingdom" (Luke 12:32).

As regards the moral life and the virtues, we note the intrinsic connection between the practice of prayer and the growth of virtues.

> [The soul improves] in all the virtues. It will continue to grow if it doesn't turn back now to offending God.[102]

As to God's service, we find the emergence of a

---

99. *Way of Perfection*, Valladolid, Chapter XXVIII:12.

100. *The Interior Castle, Fourth Dwelling Place*, Chapter III:9.

101. *Book of Her Life*, Chapter XIV:5.

102. *The Interior Castle, Fourth Dwelling Place*, Chapter III:9.

greater love, a new ardor. The expansion in God causes
a progress of love that liberates us from certain fears
of the past. In this way, filial fear gains the upper hand
over the servile fear of punishment and the fear of
losing ones health gives way to confidence in God and
the desire for mortification. In general, the soul has less
dread of ordeals.

> ...Its faith is more alive; it knows that if it suffers
> trials for God, His Majesty will give it the grace
> to suffer them with patience. Sometimes it even
> desires them because there also remains a strong
> desire to do something for God.[103]

The dilation of the soul is thus the source of fervent
apostolic desires. Nevertheless, the attainment of
this new state does not take place without an added
awareness of human frailty. Henceforward, the more the
contemplative apostle grows in friendship with the Lord
through prayer and action, the clearer things will seem
on this point.

VIII. The Fifth Dwelling Place: The Mystical Discovery of Christ

In order to illustrate the spiritual metamorphosis
that the soul undergoes in the Fifth Dwelling Place,
Teresa uses the famous image of the silkworm that is
transformed into a butterfly.

All of the efforts performed by the soul have
prepared it for building an edifice, a house, comparable
to the cocoon spun by the silkworm. More precisely, the
silkworm (the soul) has begun to live and grow thanks
to "the heat of the Holy Spirit" and the general help of
God:

> This silkworm, then, starts to live when by the heat
> of the Holy Spirit it begins to benefit through the
> general help given to us all by God and through

---

103. *The Interior Castle, Fourth Dwelling Place*, Chapter III:9.

the remedies left by Him to His Church, by going
to confession, reading good books, and hearing
sermons, which are the remedies that a soul, dead
in its carelessness, and sins [could have.] It then
begins to live and to sustain itself by these things,
and by good meditations, until it is grown. Its being
grown is what is relevant to what I'm saying ...[104]

When this silkworm is grown [...] it begins to
spin the silk and build the house wherein it will
die. I would like to point out here that this house
is Christ. Somewhere, it seems to me, I have read
or heard that our life is hidden in Christ or in God
(both are the same) or that our life is Christ.[105,106]

The concrete aspect of the image helps us understand
Teresa's thought, which at first seems a little obscure. It
means that through the soul's faithful response to the
appeals of God it deserves to be totally "lost" (in the
evangelical sense of the word) in order to find itself
again in Christ.

This radical loss of self in order to find oneself again
in Christ is experienced suddenly when the soul takes
the shortcut of the extraordinary grace of the mystical
union. In the mystical union, all of the powers are
asleep "to the things of the world and to ourselves."[107]
The soul "in every respect has died to the world so as
to live more completely in God," who is closely joined
with its "essence."[108] In the same way, the silkworm, "fat
and ugly" leaves its cocoon and becomes "a little white
butterfly, which is very pretty.[109] Because of this interior
transformation, the soul has difficulty recognizing itself.
It feels disoriented and as if it were in exile amidst the
things of this world. The little butterfly no longer knows

104. *The Interior Castle, Fifth Dwelling Place*, Chapter II:3.
105. Colossians, 11:3.
106. *The Interior Castle, Fifth Dwelling Place*, Chapter II:4.
107. *The Interior Castle, Fifth Dwelling Place*, Chapter I:3.
108. *The Interior Castle, Fifth Dwelling Place*, Chapter I:4-5.
109. *The Interior Castle, Fifth Dwelling Place*, Chapter II:2.

"where to alight and rest."[110] The divine hold on the will is such that the soul comes out of this mystical grace as if it were "sealed" by the seal of God. All of its desires are oriented toward those of God.

The grace of union constitutes the first "meeting" between the Bride and Groom, the result of which is truly the conformity of the will. Moreover, this is Teresa's most ardent wish for herself and for all those have taken the spiritual path:

> This union with God's will is the union I have desired all my life, it is the union I ask the Lord for always.[111]

Thus, the union of will is a decisive step in the identification of the soul (the bride) with Christ (the Groom). In the image of Christ, the soul feels a very painful thirst for the Redemption of all people and thus discovers from the inside the mystery of the Church, the sacrament of salvation.

In the union of will, it is thus the soul that participates with particular intensity in the charity of Christ, which embraces the entire mystical Body.

In the extraordinary "dilation" of the Fifth Dwelling Place, a qualitative threshold is crossed. It is exactly what Teresa indicated earlier when she stated that the soul no longer recognized itself.[112] The difference is due to God's customary and loving hold on the will. Recalling the sudden results of the grace of union, Teresa exclaims, "Oh greatness of God! A few years ago—and even perhaps days—this soul wasn't mindful of anything but itself. Who has placed it in the midst of such painful concerns?"[113].

---

110. *The Interior Castle, Fifth Dwelling Place*, Chapter II:8.
111. *The Interior Castle, Fifth Dwelling Place*, Chapter III:5.
112. *The Interior Castle, Fifth Dwelling Place*, Chapter II:7.
113. *The Interior Castle, Fifth Dwelling Place*, Chapter II:11.

The answer is clearly contained in the question: it is divine intervention. However, Teresa gives it a very great degree of precision. Immediately following the previous passage, she writes, "Even were we to meditate for many years we wouldn't be able to feel them as painfully as does this soul now."[114] The pain that the soul then experiences is of a different order that that which arose from intense spiritual reflection:

> Not at all, daughters, the grief that is felt here is not like that of this world. We can with God's favor, feel the grief that comes from thinking about these things a great deal, but such grief doesn't reach the intimate depths of our being as does the pain suffered in this state for it seems that the pain breaks and grinds the soul in pieces, without the soul's striving for it or even at times wanting it.[115]

In the next paragraph, Teresa explicitly attributes the anguished desires of the soul to the degree of charity that has been communicated to it:

> Haven't you heard it said of the bride [...] that God brought her into the inner wine cellar and put charity in order within her ? Since that soul now surrenders itself into His hands and its great love makes it so surrendered that it neither knows nor wants anything more than what He wants with her [...] and God desires that, without its understanding how, it may go forth from this union impressed with His seal. For indeed the soul does no more in this union than does the wax when another impresses a seal on it. The wax doesn't impress the seal upon itself ; it is only disposed—I mean by being soft. And even in order to be disposed, it doesn't soften itself but remains still and gives its consent. Oh, goodness

---

114. *The Interior Castle, Fifth Dwelling Place*, Chapter II:11.
115. *Ibid.*

> of God ; everything must be at a cost to You !
> All You want is our will and that there be no
> impediment in the wax.[116]

However, these descriptions of the fervor and
suffering of the soul should not give the impression
that this step is exclusively disquieted or dolorous. This
would be a false impression. Actually, according to St.
Teresa's own words, in the midst of these inquietudes
the soul "has never been quieter and calmer in its life."[117]
The two aspects coexist at the same time. They are
the antinomies of the spiritual life that appear once
again. The deepest participation in the life of Christ
accentuates the real tension between death and the
Resurrection, the Glory and the Cross.

The union of will gives shape to a new interior
landscape in the soul. After the mystical grace, it
experiences such intense desires "to praise the Lord, it
would want to dissolve and die a thousand deaths for
Him." It desires at the same time to undergo great trials
for him and to do penance. It desires both solitude to
be alone with God and that "all might know God." [118]
During prayer, it is racked by its desire for God, the
feeling of exile on the earth and solicitude for souls, all
the more so since it cannot bear to see to what extent
God is "offended and little esteemed in this world and
that many souls are lost, heretics as well as Moors ;
although those that grieve it most are Christians."[119]
Now that it has sprouted wings, the soul wants to act
for God, no longer a little at a time, but to the full
extent of her new capacity.[120]

God wants this grand favor of union not to be granted
in vain. In fact, so long as the small butterfly perseveres

---

116. *The Interior Castle, Fifth Dwelling Place*, Chapter II:12.
117. *The Interior Castle, Fifth Dwelling Place*, Chapter II:8.
118. *The Interior Castle, Fifth Dwelling Place*, Chapter II:7.
119. *The Interior Castle, Fifth Dwelling Place*, Chapter II:10.
120. *The Interior Castle, Fifth Dwelling Place*, Chapter II:8.

in the desire for perfection and humble distrust of itself, "it continues to live virtuously; and they catch fire from its fire."[121] And Teresa makes clear that, even if it slackens a little, this soul can, to a certain degree, continue to do good to others by "explaining the favors God grants to whoever loves and serves Him."[122]

Teresa stresses that the favor of mystical union is clearly ordered to the apostolate. The fidelity or infidelity of such a soul has a positive or negative impact on the spread of the Kingdom. To illustrate this, Teresa lists a number of biblical personages and saints. First, those "like Judas, whom the Lord calls to the apostolate by communing with them, and like Saul, whom He calls to be kings, who afterward through their own fault go astray!"[123] By falling, such souls can drag others down in their fall. This is why they are Satan's favorite target. As Teresa declares, "All hell must join for such a purpose because, as I have often said, in losing one soul of this kind, not only one is lost but a multitude."[124]

On the other hand, we have the fruitful example of the martyrs and saints such as St. Ursula, St. Dominic, St. Francis and other founders of orders. In the presence of these edifying models, Teresa asks that we meditate on "the multitude of souls God draws to Himself by means of one."[125]

Because this step in the Fifth Dwelling Place is a key step, the soul will have to endure multiple attacks from those who oppose the building of God's Kingdom.

In this period, the soul must continue to be wary of itself, to forget itself entirely and not to be exposed to temptations, for it "… is not so strong that it can place

121. *The Interior Castle, Fifth Dwelling Place*, Chapter III:1.
122. *The Interior Castle, Fifth Dwelling Place*, Chapter III:1.
123. *The Interior Castle, Fifth Dwelling Place*, Chapter III 2.
124. *The Interior Castle, Fifth Dwelling Place*, Chapter IV:6.
125. *The Interior Castle, Fifth Dwelling Place*, Chapter IV:6.

itself in the occasions (of sin) as it will be after the betrothal is made …"[126]

Therefore, it cannot settle into a false tranquility, but must always seek to move forward and to desire more than ever the perfection of love. When one has arrived at so high a place, Teresa says, it is impossible to cease to grow. Love is never idle. If it stopped, that would be "a very bad sign.[127] To assure that the soul lives truly in the union of will, Teresa recalls the infallible evangelical criterion of charity, or, as she writes, that of two wisdoms: that of love of God and that of love of neighbor.[128]

> The most certain sign, in my opinion, as to
> whether or not we are observing these two laws
> is whether we observe well the love of neighbor.
> We cannot know whether or not we love
> God, although there are strong indications for
> recognizing that we do love Him; but we can know
> whether we love our neighbor. And be certain that
> the more advanced you will be in the love of God,
> for the love His Majesty has for us is so great that
> to repay us for our love of neighbor He will in a
> thousand ways increase the love we have for Him.
> I cannot doubt this.[129]

> I believe that, since our nature is bad, we will not
> reach perfection in the love of neighbor if that
> love doesn't rise from love of God as its root. [130]

IX. The Sixth Dwelling Place: «Where the Soul Now Wounded With Love for Its Spouse Resides»

> Well then, let us, with the help of the Holy Spirit,
> speak of the sixth dwelling places, where the soul
> is now wounded with love for its Spouse and

---

126. *The Interior Castle, Fifth Dwelling Place*, Chapter IV:5.
127. *The Interior Castle, Fifth Dwelling Place*, Chapter IV:10.
128. *The Interior Castle, Fifth Dwelling Place*, Chapter III:7.
129. *The Interior Castle, Fifth Dwelling Place*, Chapter III:8.
130. *The Interior Castle, Fifth Dwelling Place*, Chapter III:9.

strives for more opportunities to be alone and, in
conformity with its state, to rid itself of everything
that can be an obstacle to this solitude. That
meeting left such an impression that the soul's
whole desire is to enjoy it again.[131]

Thus St. Teresa introduces her readers to the Sixth
Dwelling Place, which is characterized by spiritual
betrothal. The new state engenders in the person an
intrinsic and total docility to the divine will. This is why
one can speak in this regard of a certain perfection of
the contemplative apostolate. Here we have a soul "now
wounded with love for its Spouse," which, in the Sixth
Dwelling Place, is deeply purified and transformed by
it. Now the soul desires more and more intensely the
perfect realization of the union.

The meeting which took place in the Fifth Dwelling
Place has created in it the burning desire to finally
celebrate the betrothal. The Bridegroom will use this
aspiration itself to purify it, for He "wants it to desire
this more, and He wants the betrothal to take place at a
cost."[132]

In a veiled form, there is an allusion to the "interior
and exterior trials"[133] that the soul will have to face
in order to finally penetrate into the seventh and last
dwelling place, where the spiritual marriage, a symbolic
expression of the identification with Christ, will finally
be realized. As in the real world, the betrothal is thus
a preparation for marriage, these two moments being
closely connected with each other. Teresa emphasizes
this connection at the supernatural level: "And this goes
for many other things that take place in this state—I
mean in these two dwelling places, for there is no closed

---

131. *The Interior Castle, Sixth Dwelling Place*, Chapter I:1.
132. *Ibidem.*
133. *Ibidem.*

door between the one and the other."[134] Nevertheless,
"because there are things in the last [dwelling place]
that are not revealed to those who have not yet reached
it,"[135] Teresa has chosen to distinguish them, while still
affirming this spiritual circulation between them.

Let us note here Teresa's reference to "interior and
exterior trials" typical to this moment in the spiritual
life.

Teresa mentions two major kinds of trials, called
"exterior." First, the criticisms and persecutions that
come from more or less well intentioned acquaintances,
both close and distant.

> I want to begin with the smallest trial. There is
> an outcry by persons a Sister is dealing with and
> even by those she does not deal with and who,
> it seems to her, would never even think of her;
> gossip like the following: "She's trying to make out
> she's a saint; she goes to extremes to deceive the
> world and bring others to ruin ; there are other
> better Christians who don't put on all this outward
> show." (And it's worth noting that she is not
> putting on any outward show but striving to fulfill
> well her state in life.) Those she considered her
> friends turn away from her, and they are the ones
> who take the largest and most painful bite at her:
> "That soul has gone away and is clearly mistaken ;
> these are things of the devil ; she will turn out
> like this person or that other that went astray, and
> will bring about a decline in virtue ; she deceived
> her confessors." And they go to these confessors,
> telling them so, giving them examples of what
> happened to some that were lost in this way; a
> thousand kinds of ridicule and statements like the
> above.[136]

---

134. *The Interior Castle, Sixth Dwelling Place*, Chapter IV:4.
135. *Ibidem.*
136. *The Interior Castle, Sixth Dwelling Place*, Chapter I:3.

Second, there are serious illnesses:

> The Lord is wont also to send it the severest
> illnesses. This is a much greater trial, especially
> when the pains are acute. For in some way, if these
> pains are severe, the trial is, it seems to me, the
> greatest on earth—I mean the greatest exterior
> trial, however many the other pains. I say "if the
> pains are severe" because they then afflict the
> soul interiorly and exteriorly in such a way that
> it doesn't know what to do with itself. It would
> willingly accept at once any martyrdom rather than
> these sharp pains.[137]

As to the interior trials, they may be reduced to three
main ones. First of all, there are those that come from
the incomprehension of confessors, leaving the soul
in great internal distress and solitude. The second
great interior trial comes from the hidden activity of
the Devil which obscures understanding, acts on the
imagination and suggests to it crazy ideas, such as being
reproved by God, for example. This kind of action
overflows into one's feelings. The third trial that works
on the soul comes from the crushing experience of its
troubles, its emptiness and its helplessness to do any
good.[138] The memory of its sins so obsesses it, "grace is
so hidden that not even a very tiny spark is visible. The
soul doesn't think that it has any love of God or that it
ever had any."[139]

St. Teresa's life is a living illustration of these kinds
of trials.[140] As to the other kind of affliction, that of
illnesses, we know that throughout her life St. Teresa
was besieged by illness. She confides them to us very
quietly, speaking in the third person:

> I know a person who cannot truthfully say that

---

137. *The Interior Castle, Sixth Dwelling Place*, Chapter I:6.
138. *The Interior Castle, Sixth Dwelling Place*, Chapter I:10-11.
139. *The Interior Castle, Sixth Dwelling Place*, Chapter I:11.
140. *Book of Her Life*, Chapter XXX-XXXI.

> from the time the Lord began forty years ago to
> grant the favor that was mentioned she spent even
> one day without pains and other kinds of suffering
> (from lack of bodily health, I mean) and other
> great trials.[141]

("Forty years ago" refers to time of the grace of
mystical union with which she was favored during the
early years of her religious life.)

This rather grim picture is made brighter, despite all,
by sudden glimpses of light.

> In sum, there is no remedy in this tempest but to
> wait for the mercy of God. For at an unexpected
> time, with one word alone or a chance happening,
> He so quickly calms the storm that it seems there
> had not been even as much as a cloud in that soul,
> and it remains filled with sunlight and much more
> consolation.[142]

All this reminds the soul that it is firmly in the hands
of God's mercy, which employs all human means,
human weakness and even the action of Satan to purify
and transform it. St. Teresa makes clear that the torment
comes from on high. The soul will come out of the
melting pot of suffering "more refined and purified, so
as to see the Lord within itself."[143]

> Our great God wants us to know our own misery
> and that He is king; and this is very important for
> what lies ahead.[144]

That which will follow, says Teresa, is first of
all betrothal, then spiritual marriage, very elevated
conditions in which the soul, having become perfectly
humble, is capable of receiving the full measure of love
with which divine mercy wishes to fill it.

141. *The Interior Castle, Sixth Dwelling Place*, Chapter I:7.
142. *The Interior Castle, Sixth Dwelling Place*, Chapter I:10.
143. *Book of Her Life*, Chapter XXX:40.
144. *The Interior Castle, Sixth Dwelling Place*, Chapter I:12.

1) The Love That Fills: The Spiritual Betrothal

Before the soul unites completely with God, "He (the Bridegroom) makes it desire Him vehemently by certain delicate means the soul itself does not understand... These are impulses so delicate and refined, for they proceed from very deep within the interior part of the soul, that I don't know any comparison that will fit," St. Teresa writes.[145] Thus, she indicates the means used by the Lord to awaken the soul to more love and hence to prepare it for the union of the betrothed by purifying and illuminating it. The senses and the powers are suspended. They are "so absorbed that we can say they are dead."[146] "What I know in this case is that the soul was never so awake to the things of God nor did it have such deep enlightenment and knowledge of His Majesty."[147] In its rapture, during which the betrothal is sealed, it is as if the soul were raised to God, who "begins to show it the things of the kingdom that He prepared for it."[148] The soul can in no way resist this transport. It no longer belongs to itself, It feels carried away in its spirit "as easily as a huge giant snatches up a straw."[149]

It is important to note in this regard that the first rapture with which St. Teresa was favored had the immediate effect of detaching her heart from friendships and orienting it exclusively toward God and toward those who serve Him. In the course of this rapture, she heard these words: "No longer do I want you to converse with men but with angels."[150]

Exclusive attachment to God and disappropriation of all things are, as it were, the two sides of this spiritual

---

145. *The Interior Castle, Sixth Dwelling Place*, Chapter II:1.
146. *The Interior Castle, Sixth Dwelling Place*, Chapter IV:4.
147. *Ibidem.*
148. *Book of Her Life*, Chapter XX:2.
149. *The Interior Castle, Sixth Dwelling Place*, Chapter V:2.
150. *Book of Her Life*, Chapter XXIV:5.

condition. The extraordinary favors, such as visions, for example, contribute, for their part, to reinforcing this basic state. See, for example, chapter VIII:3 of the Sixth Dwelling Place, where the mental vision of Christ maintains in the soul "continued desires to please God," together with "so much contempt for everything that does not bring it to Him."

In the dazzling light of God, all created things take on their true substance. Thus, for example, in a mental vision, Teresa saw "all things … in God and how He has them all in Himself."[151] The higher elevated are the favors, the more the soul forgets itself and is lost in a very profound abnegation of itself. The desire to enjoy, praise and serve God increase to the same degree. This is why she feels all the more obliged not to be ungrateful and to desire to content God "in all things."[152]

However, the soul is aware that, in its response of love and in its works, it will always be indebted because God's gifts are absolutely free. The more it serves God, the more it knows that it is indebted to God, because it has understood by experience that it can do nothing through itself, but only through God's gift to it. Love calls forth love. The free gift begets free service: "Freely you received, freely give."[153]

2) The Love That Becomes a Servant

Thus, the Sixth Dwelling Place sees the triumph of love in the soul. Completely taken over by God, having become "His own and His spouse, He begins showing it some little part of the kingdom that it has gained by being espoused to Him."[154]

In the end, the important fact is this reciprocal co-

---

151   *The Interior Castle, Sixth Dwelling Place*, Chapter X:2.
152   *The Interior Castle, Sixth Dwelling Place*, Chapter II:5.
153   Matthew 10:8.
154   *The Interior Castle, Sixth Dwelling Place*, Chapter IV:9..

penetration of God and the soul, which now belongs to God totally. The more or less extraordinary mystical phenomena that may occur then all work to support this union. Every step forward in the union corresponds to a soul that is more docile to the motions of the Holy Spirit. Henceforward, the soul is summoned to the union of spiritual marriage. This is the reason the Lord does not give anyone the right to meddle with it. "Well and good if its body, or honor, or possessions are touched," but not the soul. If the soul should grow distant from Him "through a very culpable boldness, He will protect it from the whole world and even from all hell."[155]

While it belongs to God, the soul remains free. Thus, it may fall, but now the gifts of God (particularly the knowledge of self, which is the source of true humility) offer powerful support to its faithfulness.

Henceforward, the soul thirsts to "satisfy love, and it is love's nature to serve with deeds in a thousand ways."[156]

The soul now understands clearly and in a renewed way that this burning love of God that consumes it is exactly the same as the love that permits the martyrs to give the testimony of blood.[157] This is why it intensely desires to be associated with the sufferings of Christ.

If love fills those it conquers with strength, we have also seen in the Sixth Dwelling Place to what point it pursues in them its work of purification. It is for this reason that the mystical "little butterfly" still suffers, because it cannot manage to find its stability, pulled as it is by its contradictory desires to escape the world in order to see our Lord and "to enter into the midst of

---

155   *The Interior Castle, Sixth Dwelling Place*, Chapter IV:16.

156. *The Interior Castle, Sixth Dwelling Place*, Chapter IX:18.

157. *The Interior Castle, Sixth Dwelling Place*, Chapter IV:15.

the world to try to play a part in getting even one soul to praise God more."[158] The desires to see God are now so intense that the soul is deeply wounded by them. It is a suffering of purification, of purgatory,[159] that prepares the soul for the spiritual marriage. Sometimes, "while this soul is going about in this manner, burning up within itself, a blow is felt from elsewhere (the soul doesn't understand from where or how). The blow comes often through a sudden thought or word about death's delay."[160]

3) The Example of Moses as an Illustration of Teresa's Experience

In chapter IV of the Sixth Dwelling Place, the person of Moses is evoked with regard to the different kinds of visions (imaginary and intellectual) that may come to the soul.[161] Speaking of intellectual visions, Teresa states that it is possible, though difficult or sometimes even practically impossible, to describe visions of this kind. Everything depends on their degree of elevation.[162] To illustrate her words, she cites the example of Jacob's vision of the ladder[163] and Moses' vision of the burning bush.[164] Let us listen to her present this last example:

> Nor did Moses know how to describe all that he saw in the bush, but only what God wished him to describe. But if God had not shown secrets to his soul along with a certitude that made him recognize and believe that they were from God, Moses could not have entered into so many severe trials. But he must have understood such deep things among the thorns of that bush that the vision gave him the courage to do what he did for

---

158. *The Interior Castle, Sixth Dwelling Place*, Chapter VI:1-4.
159. *The Interior Castle, Sixth Dwelling Place*, Chapter XI:3-6.
160. *The Interior Castle, Sixth Dwelling Place*, Chapter XI:2.
161. *The Interior Castle, Sixth Dwelling Place*, Chapter IV:7.
162. *The Interior Castle, Sixth Dwelling Place*, Chapter IV:5.
163. Genesis 28:12; *The Interior Castle, Sixth Dwelling Place*, Chapter IV:6.
164. Exodus 3:2.

the people of Israel.[165]

These lines establish a very clear relationship between
the founding vision of the burning bush and Moses'
future role. It is actually in this extraordinary vision that
his mission as leader of the people of Israel is rooted,
which will inspire his actions through which God will
liberate the people, seal the covenant and give them
the divine law. In fact, it is in the revealed Name of the
Lord that Moses will present himself to the Israelites
and speak to them. This is also the Name that later
will prove to them the authenticity of the message of
liberation. The miracles accompanying this will confirm
the active presence of the Lord and the truth of His
words, "I will be with you."[166]

The first and greatest of these miracles was certainly
the "deep things" that the Lord communicated to Moses
and "gave him the courage to do what he did for the
people of Israel." These "deep things" counterbalance,
in the words of Teresa, the "many severe trials" he had
to endure. Thus, at the foundation of the mission of
this great friend of God lies a spiritual experience that is
quite extraordinary and one that is in proportion to the
work that he is asked to carry out. This very profound
contemplative knowledge of God gives him the light
and the strength to overcome all obstacles.

Thus, the episode of the vision of the burning bush
permits Teresa of Jesus to stress the powerful help
that certain extraordinary favors can provide in the
realization of the apostolate. She admits that, "without
this strength she would have been unable to suffer such
great trials, contradictions, and sicknesses, which have
been without number. And it happens that she is never
without some kind of suffering."[167]

165. *The Interior Castle, Sixth Dwelling Place*, Chapter IV:7.
166. Exodus 3:16 ff.
167. *Spiritual Testimonies*, Seville, 1575.

Among the blessings with which Teresa was endowed, special mention should be given to the transverberation of her heart, which resulted in her particular apostolic fruitfulness.

The description of this wound of love is given to us in greater detail in the autobiography and in the *Interior Castle*.[168] In the story of her life, she mentions the intervention of an angel: "in his hands a large golden dart and at the end of the iron tip there appeared to be a little fire." She continues: "It seemed to me this angel plunged the dart several times into my heart and that it reached deep within me. When he drew it out, I thought he was carrying off with him the deepest part of me ; and he left me all on fire with great love of God."[169]

According the St. John of the Cross, this was a very high grace of spiritual fruitfulness that is conferred on those who are destined to have a spiritual posterity. He comments:

> Few persons have reached these heights. Some have, however, especially those whose virtue and spirit were to be diffused among their children. With respect to the first fruits of the spirit, God accords to founders wealth and value commensurate with the greater or lesser following they will have in their doctrine and spirituality.[170]

The transverberation is the external manifestation of God's hold on Teresa's soul. By conferring on her "wealth and value commensurate with the greater or lesser following" of her disciples, it makes her a powerful leader of souls. Thus, this new and considerable infusion of love gives the soul a particular effectiveness and at the same time marks it for a specific

---

168. *Book of Her Life*, Chapitre XXIX:10, 13 ; *The Interior Castle, Sixth Dwelling Place*, Chapter II:4.

169. *Book of Her Life*, Chapter XXIX, § 13.

170. *The Living Flame of Love*, strophe 2.

mission. What actually counts – and this is true for all of the spiritual life –is that the divine reality is infused and experienced by the soul and not the way that this is transmitted to it. If a soul is led by the privileged means of a "favor so sublime" as the grace of transverberation, it can only be obliged to "strive to better its entire life, and to serve."[171]

X. In the Seventh Dwelling Place: The Summit of the Union With God: The Spiritual Union and the Spiritual Marriage

By penetrating into the Seventh Dwelling Place, the soul enters into the deepest center of itself, into the "the main dwelling place where the very secret exchanges between God and the soul take place."[172] It is here that it contracts spiritual marriage with God. In a Spiritual Testimony of 1571, Teresa recounts how a mental vision of the Blessed Trinity marked her entry into this last dwelling place:

> On the Tuesday following Ascension Thursday, having remained a while in prayer after Communion, I was grieved because I was so distracted I couldn't concentrate. So I complained to the Lord about our miserable nature. My soul began to enkindle, and it seemed to me I knew clearly in an intellectual vision that the entire Blessed Trinity was present. In this state my soul understood by a certain kind of representation (like an illustration of the truth), in such a way that my dullness could perceive, how God is three and one. And so it seemed that all three Persons were represented distinctly in my soul and that they spoke to me, telling me that from this day I would see an improvement in myself in respect to three things and that each one of these Persons

---

171. *The Interior Castle, Sixth Dwelling Place*, Chapter II:5.
172. *The Interior Castle, First Dwelling Place*, Chapter I:3.

would grant me a favor: one, the favor of charity;
another, the favor of being able to suffer gladly;
and the third, the favor of experiencing this charity
with an enkindling in the soul. I understood
those words the Lord spoke, that the three divine
Persons would be with the soul in grace; for I saw
them within myself in the way described.[173]

After describing her entry into the Seventh Dwelling
Place, Teresa recounts in great detail the grace of
spiritual marriage that she received in the days around
November 18, 1572. The event is reported to us in
two texts: a Spiritual Testimony and a passage from
the Seventh Dwelling Place.[174] The text of the Spiritual
Testimony is very rich in specific details. Here is an
extract:

Then He [the resurrected Christ] appeared to me
in an imaginative vision, as at other times, very
interiorly, and He gave me His right hand and said:
"Behold this nail; it is a sign you will be My bride
from today on. Until now you have not merited
this; from now on not only will you look after My
honor as being the honor of our Creator, King,
and God, but you will look after it as My true
bride. My honor is yours, and yours Mine."

The union that results from this state of spiritual
marriage is complete and final (unlike the condition of
betrothal) and thus stable. It sees itself admitted into the
continual society of the Holy Trinity:

Here all three Persons communicate themselves to
it, speak to it, and explain those words of the Lord
in the Gospel: that He and the Father and the
Holy Spirit will come to dwell with the soul that
loves Him and keeps His commandments.[175]

---

173. *Spiritual Testimonies.*
174. *Spiritual Testimonies*, 1572, Incarnación, Avila; *The Interior Castle,
Seventh Dwelling Place*, Chapter I:1.
175. *The Interior Castle, Seventh Dwelling Place*, Chapter I:6.

The soul will never lose this divine company, but it will not always be equally luminous, because at certain times, as the saint says, "a person who, after being in a bright room with others, finds himself, once the shutters are closed, in darkness."[176] However, throughout everything, it remains conscious of the divine presence.

From now on it can be both Martha and Mary. External concerns will no longer turn it away from its God.

> Such was the experience of this person, for in everything she found herself improved, and it seemed to her, despite the trials she underwent and the business affairs she had to attend to, that the essential part of her soul never moved from that room. As a result, it seemed to her that there was, in a certain way, a division in her soul. And while suffering some great trials a little after God granted her this favor, she complained of that part of the soul, as Martha complained of Mary,[177] and sometimes pointed out that it was there always enjoying the quietude at its own pleasure while leaving her in the midst of so many trials and occupations that she could not keep it company. [178]

In the Seventh Dwelling Place, certain gifts are given that perfect the transformation of the soul.

Christ reveals Himself in His humanity in the most intimate center of the soul and unites with the soul in a perpetual bond.

> One can say no more—insofar as can be understood—than that the soul, I mean the spirit, is made one with God. For since His majesty is also spirit, He has wished to show His love for us by giving some persons understanding of the point to which this love reaches so that we might

---

176. *The Interior Castle, Seventh Dwelling Place*, Chapter I:9.
177. Luke 10:40.
178. *The Interior Castle, Seventh Dwelling Place*, Chapter I:10.

praise His grandeur. For He has desired to be so joined with the creature that, just as those who are married cannot be separated, He doesn't want to be separated from the soul.

The spiritual betrothal is different, for the two often separate. And the union is also different because, even though it is the joining of two things into one, in the end the two can be separated and each remains by itself. We observe this ordinarily, for the favor of union with the Lord passes quickly, and afterward the soul remains without that company ; I mean without awareness of it. In this other favor from the Lord, no. The soul always remains with its God in that center. Let us say that the union is like the joining of two wax candles to such an extent that the flame coming from them is but one, or that the wick, the flame, and the wax are all one. But afterward one candle can be easily separated from the other and there are two candles ; the same holds for the wick. In the spiritual marriage the union is like what we have when rain falls from the sky into a river or fount ; all is water, for the rain that fell from heaven cannot be divided or separated from the water of the river. Or it is like what we have when a little stream enters the sea, there is no means of separating the two.

Perhaps this is what St. Paul means in saying *He that is joined or united to the Lord becomes one spirit with him.*[179] And he also says, *Mihi vivere Christus est, mori lucrum* [For me to live is Christ, to die is gain]. The soul as well, I think, can say these words now because this state is the place where the little butterfly we mentioned dies, and with the greatest joy because its life is now Christ.[180]

When Teresa wants to give an idea of this new life

---

179. Corinthians 6:17.
180. *The Interior Castle, Seventh Dwelling Place*, Chapter II:3-4 and 5.

that she feels overflowing within herself, a tumultuous profusion of symbols, an abundance of depictions flow from her pen!

> Through some secret aspirations the soul understands clearly that it is God who gives life to our soul. These aspirations come very, very often in such a living way that they can in no way be doubted. The soul feels them very clearly even though they are indescribable. But the feeling is so powerful that sometimes the soul cannot avoid the loving expressions they cause, such as: O Life of my life ! Sustenance that sustains me ! and things of this sort. For from those divine breasts where it seems God is always sustaining the soul there flow streams of milk bringing comfort to all the people of the castle. It seems the Lord desires that in some manner these others in the castle may enjoy the great deal the soul is enjoying and that from that full-flowing river, where this tiny fount is swallowed up, a spurt of that water will sometimes be directed toward the sustenance of those who in corporeal things must serve these two who are wed [...] For just as a great gush of water could not reach us if it didn't have a source [...] it is understood clearly that there is Someone in the interior depths who shoots these arrows and gives life to this life, and that there is a Sun in the interior of the soul from which a brilliant light proceeds and is sent to the faculties. The soul [...] does not move from that center nor is its peace lost.[181]

The mystical union with Christ is not defined simply by the delights that accompany it, but by the communion with the sufferings of the Redeemer. In the *Way of Perfection*, Teresa exhorts her sisters to keep company with Christ through prayer, looking on him with faith, becoming accustomed to walking at his side

---

181. *The Interior Castle, Seventh Dwelling Place*, Chapter II:6.

"stumbling, falling with him under the weight of the Cross."[182] The same recommendation returns now in *The Interior Castle*. Here it is more general and concerns the Christian existence as a whole, i.e. not only the life of prayer, but also the apostolic life. In the famous chapter VII of the Sixth Dwelling Place, which is specifically devoted to the central place of Christ's Humanity in the spiritual life, Teresa invites all Christians not to turn away from the good company of Jesus (nor that of His Most Blessed Mother). "Life is long, and there are in it many trials, and we need to look at Christ our model, how He suffered them, and also at His apostles and saints so as to bear these trials with perfection."[183] Moreover, Teresa notes that those who were most favored by Christ because they lived closest to Him, such as the glorious Mother and the glorious Apostles, as well as St. Paul, had to undergo the greatest trials.[184]

In the same chapter of the Seventh Dwelling Place, which represents the culminating point of spiritual growth, stress is again placed on the need to contribute to the work of salvation by sharing the sufferings of Christ, without dwelling too much on the delights brought by the perfect union. Evidence of this is a well known passage that is worth citing at some length:

> Fix your eyes on the Crucified and everything will become small for you. If His Majesty showed us His love by means of such works and frightful torments, how is it you want to please Him only with words? Do you know what it means to be truly spiritual? It means becoming the slaved of God. Marked with His brand, which is that of the cross, spiritual persons, because now they have given Him their liberty, can be sold by Him as slaves of everyone, as He was. He doesn't thereby

---

182. *Escorial Manuscript,* Chapter 42:7.

183. *The Interior Castle, Sixth Dwelling Place*, Chapter VII:13.

184. *The Interior Castle, Seventh Dwelling Place*, Chapter IV:5.

do them any harm or grant them a small favor.[185]

All of these texts fully demonstrate that the elevated states of union with God and with Christ, and particularly the spiritual marriage, lead ipso facto to Redemption. The life of prayer or the mystical life has as its purpose "works" and it gives us the strength to accomplish them.

Conversely, the works confirm the authenticity of the mystical life. This is why Teresa emphasizes, "This is the reason for prayer, my daughters, the purpose of this spiritual marriage: the birth always of good works, good works."[186]

Thus, the very dynamism of the spiritual marriage compels us toward works, for love is always in movement and never the same. "I hold that love, where present, cannot possibly be constant while remaining always the same."[187] It is never idle:

> That the faculties, senses, and all the corporeal will not be idle, the soul wages more war from the center than it did when it was outside suffering with them, for then it didn't understand the tremendous gain trials bring. Perhaps they were the means by which God brought it to the center, and the company it has gives it much greater strength than ever.[188]

Love is always fruitful, like God from which it emanates.

Christian charity is defined by this movement of love. It does stop here in the enjoyment of contemplation, but is extended by works. Works are at the same time the sign of the union and of the quality of the love in the soul. And only a look of faith and love constantly

---

185. *The Interior Castle, Seventh Dwelling Place*, Chapter IV:8.
186. *The Interior Castle, Seventh Dwelling Place*, Chapter IV:6.
187. *The Interior Castle, Seventh Dwelling Place*, Chapter IV:9.
188. *The Interior Castle, Seventh Dwelling Place*, Chapter IV:10.

cast on the Crucified Christ allows us to discover how far the demands of charity can lead.

Drawing ceaselessly from the Trinitarian source, the mystical apostle is thus perfectly convinced that the power of fruitfulness that impregnates action does not come from oneself but from God who is present and active within. This conviction keeps humility alive and well, all the more so since the individual continues to experience at the same time human weakness. The person then experiences a strange paradox that overflows from the concomitant feeling of the presence of the Trinity within and of the human and spiritual poverty. To paint a true portrait of the soul in this Seventh Dwelling Place, it is necessary to go a little more deeply into this apparently disconcerting antinomy.

Sometimes, when it arrives at the spiritual marriage, the soul is particularly sensitive to its wretchedness. It feels itself poor in the face of the vastness of the design of God's love and the magnitude of the task of Redemption. In God's light, it sees the little service that it renders to God and, with regard to outside works, "rather the soul's pain lies in seeing that what it can now do by its own efforts amounts to nothing."[189] Quite the contrary, however, this feeling of inadequacy does not hinder its confidence that God will manifest the divine presence, since now the interior dialog with God is permanent and God fills the soul with strength when it needs it. Even at the summit of the mystical union, the apostles must still and always experience their poverty through labors and sufferings. Despite the presence of the Trinity, "the cross is not wanting but it doesn't disquiet or make them lose peace," because "the presence of the Lord [...] makes them soon forget everything."[190]

---

189. *The Interior Castle, Seventh Dwelling Place*, Chapter III:3.
190. *The Interior Castle, Seventh Dwelling Place*, Chapter III:15.

Recommended Carmelite Websites

**For more information about the Carmelites today,
our spirituality and our ministries worldwide, visit:**
carmelites.net
ocarm.org
carmelites.info
ocarm-ocd.org

For a listing of Carmelite provinces worldwide, visit:m

For a listing of Monasteries of Carmelite nuns, visit:
carmelites.info/nuns

For a listing of Carmelite Hermitages, please visit:
carmelites.info/hermits

For a listing of sites about Lay Carmelites:
carmelites.info/lay carmel

For a listing of Affiliated Congregations and Institutes:
carmelites.info/congregations

**For more information about our work
with the United Nations, visit:**
carmelitengo.org

**For more information about other publications
available from the Carmelites, visit:**
carmelites.info/publications
icspublications.org